This coloring book is a vibrant, life-filled adventure especially dedicated to you and your incredible creative journeys! Let each page be an invitation to explore an enchanted world, full of fascinating animals and exuberant colors.

May every stroke of your pencil be a colorful smile, illuminating not only the figures in this book, but also your heart full of imagination. May the joy of coloring be like a rainbow of possibilities, providing moments of fun, learning and discovery.

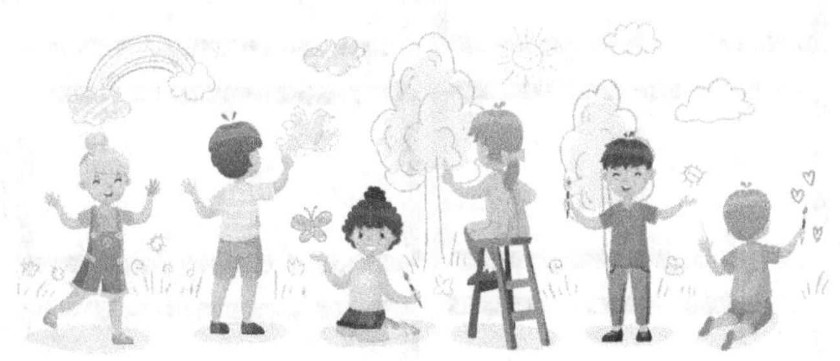

Josiel Oliver 2024

Teste Color Page

Here begins the story of a new artist

↓ SIGN YOUR NAME HERE ↓

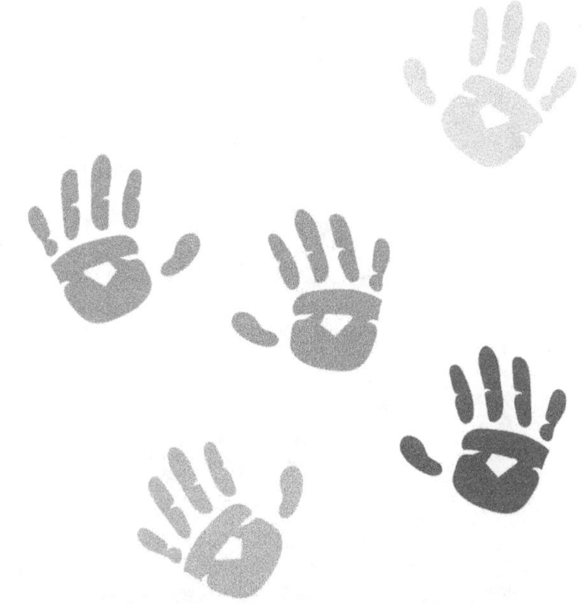

This book belong to:

____

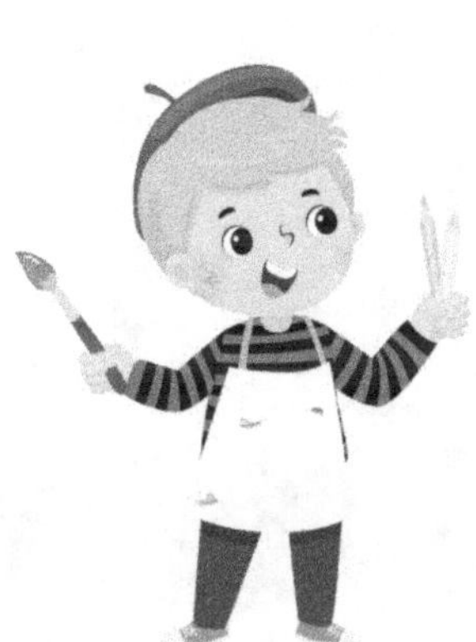

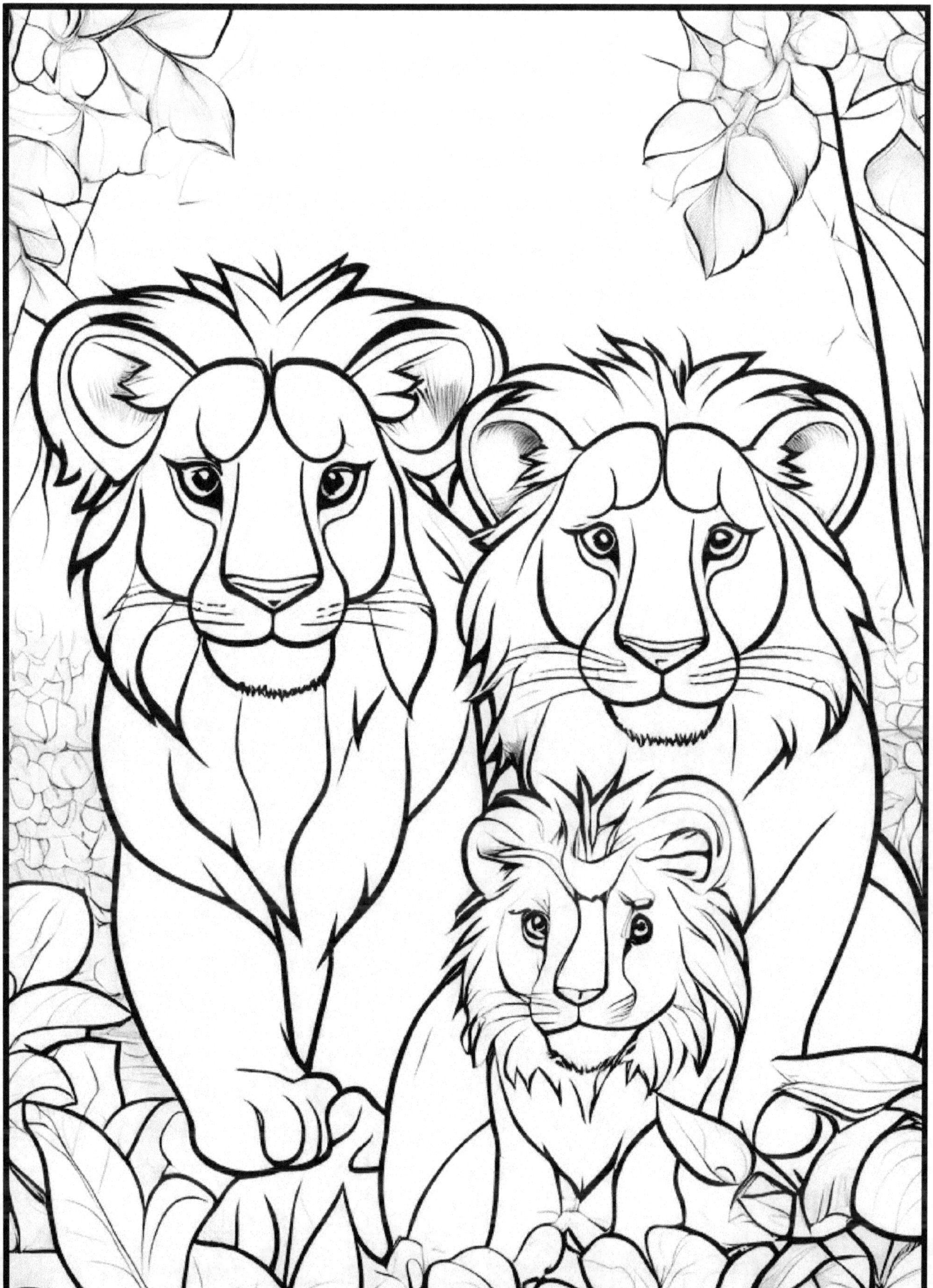

elephant

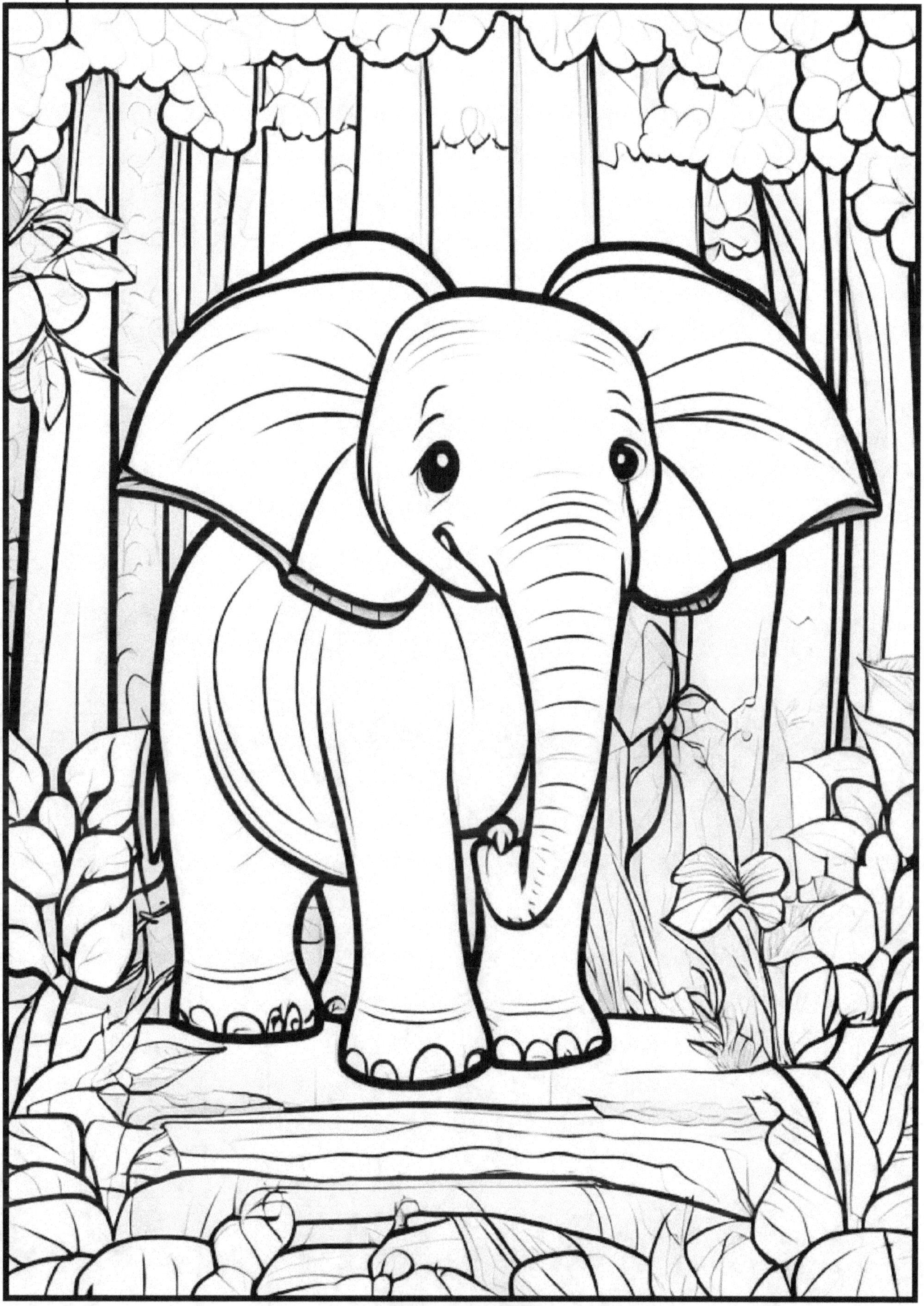

macaw

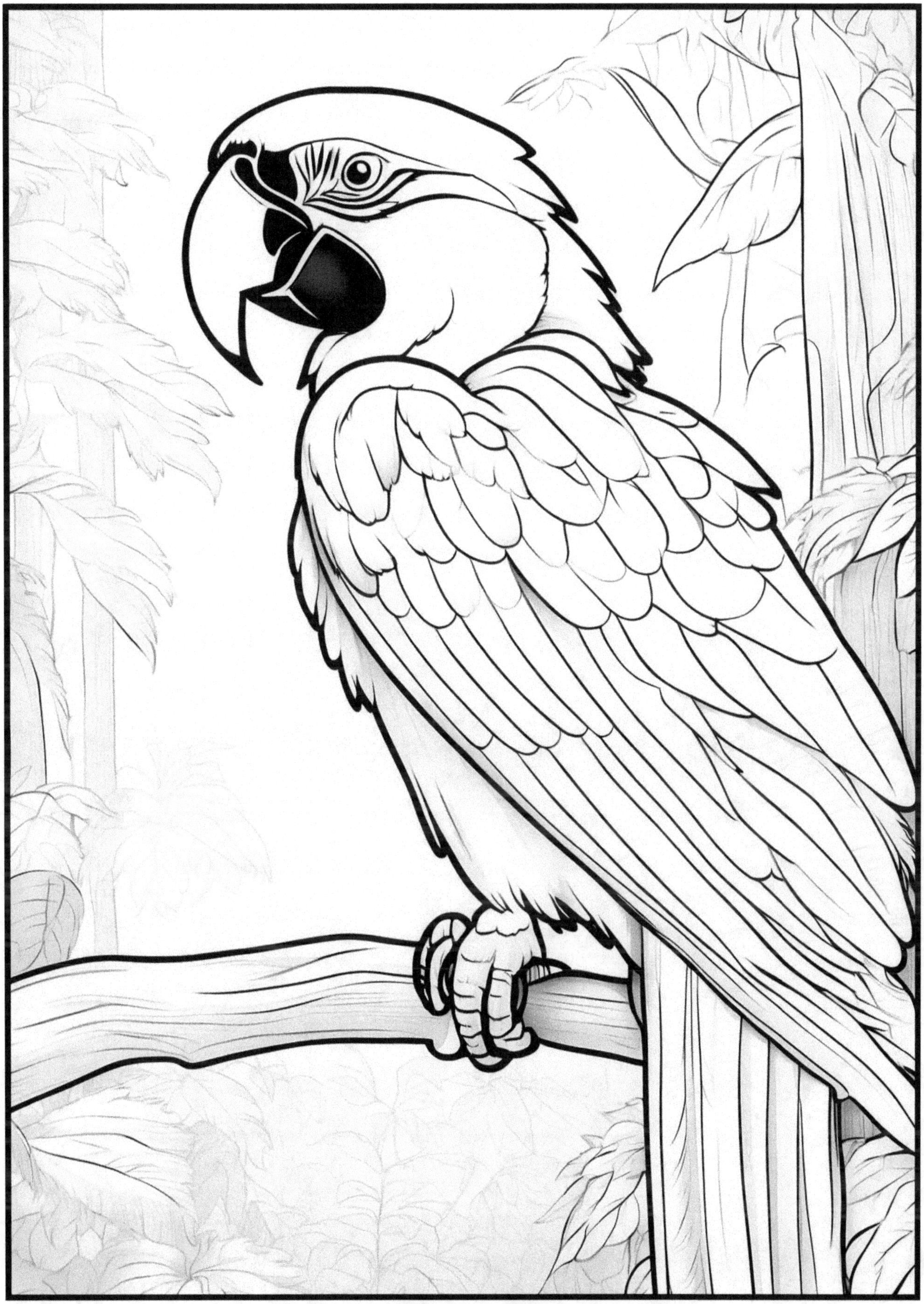

monkey

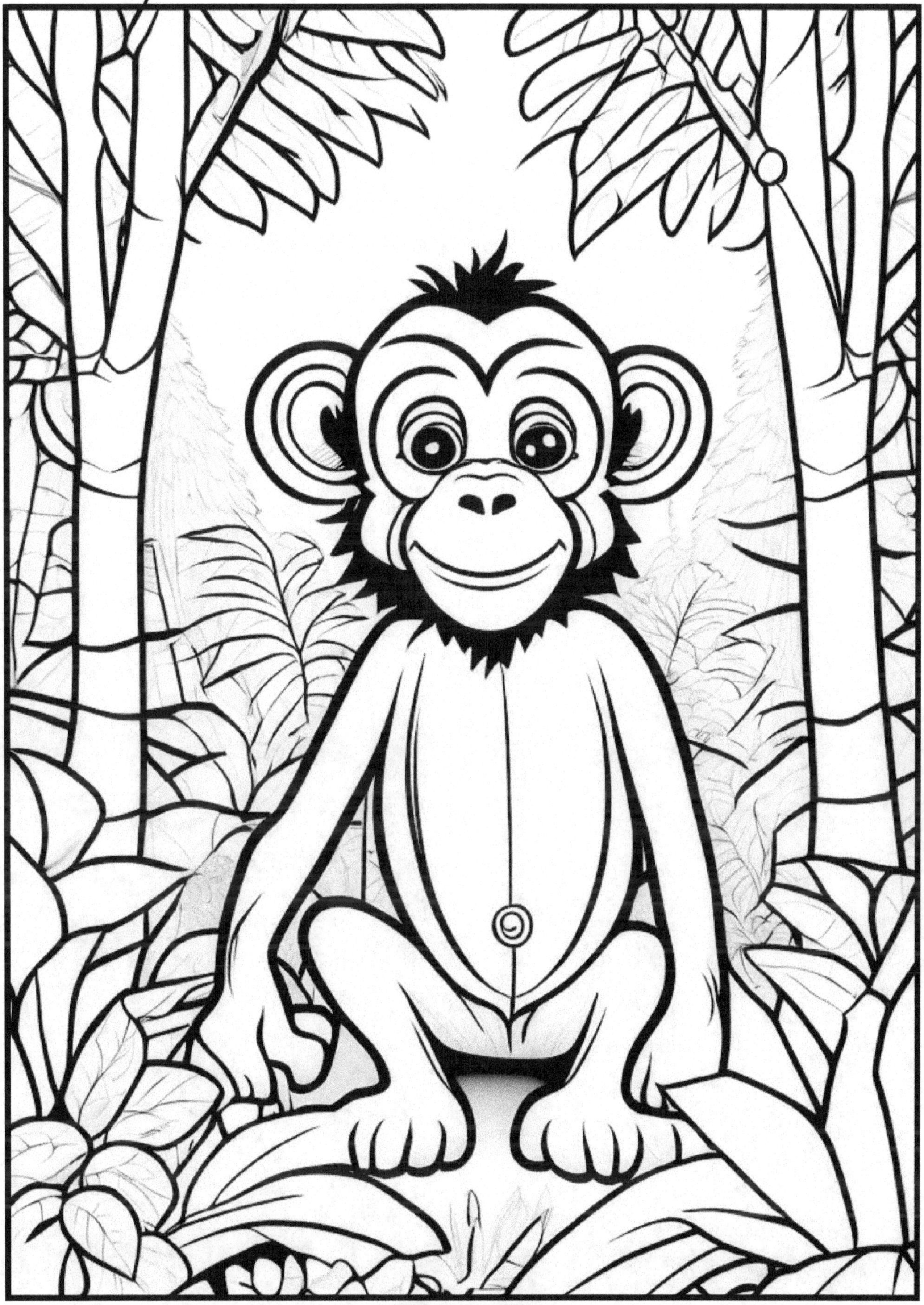

macaw

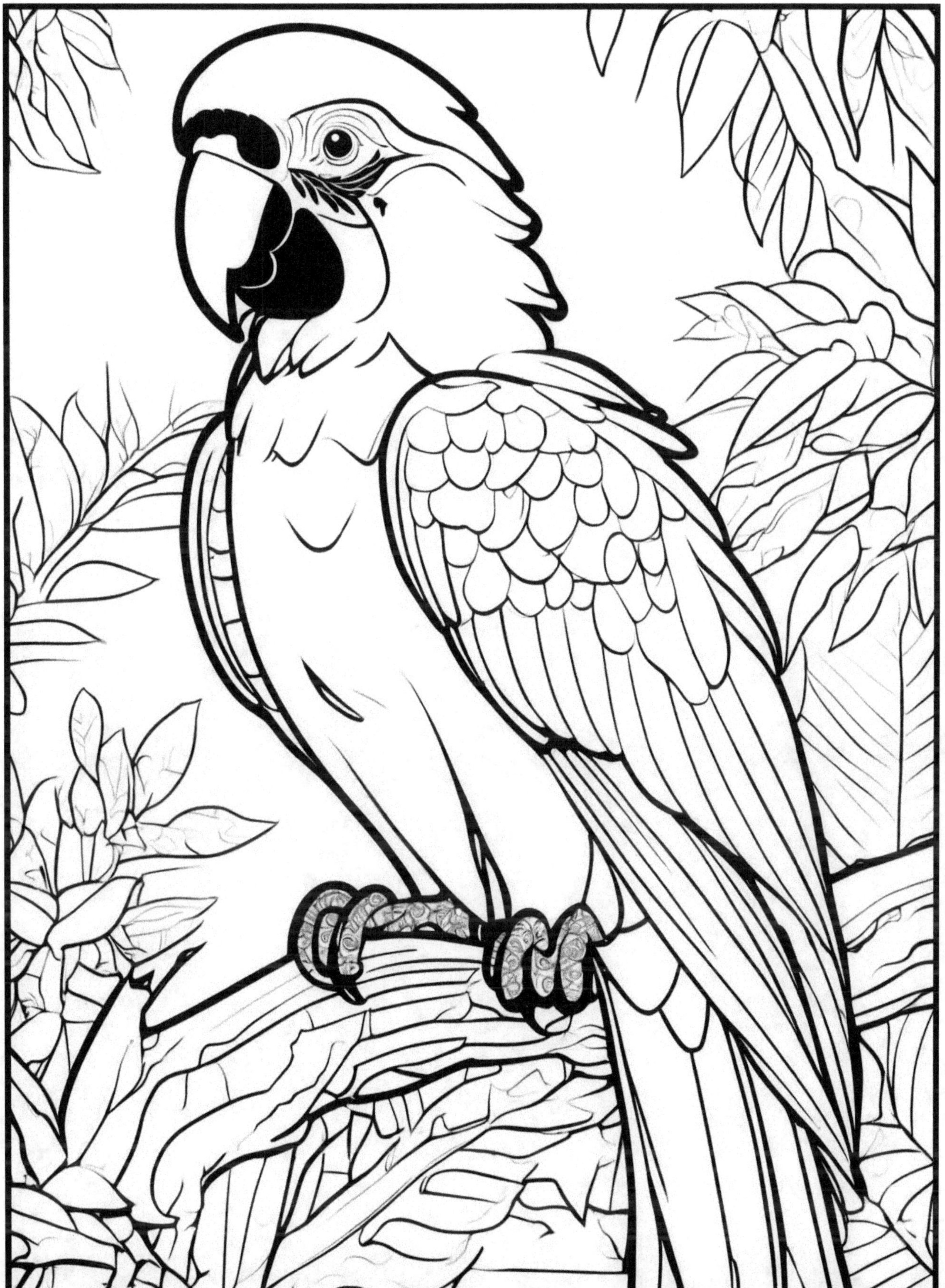

zebra

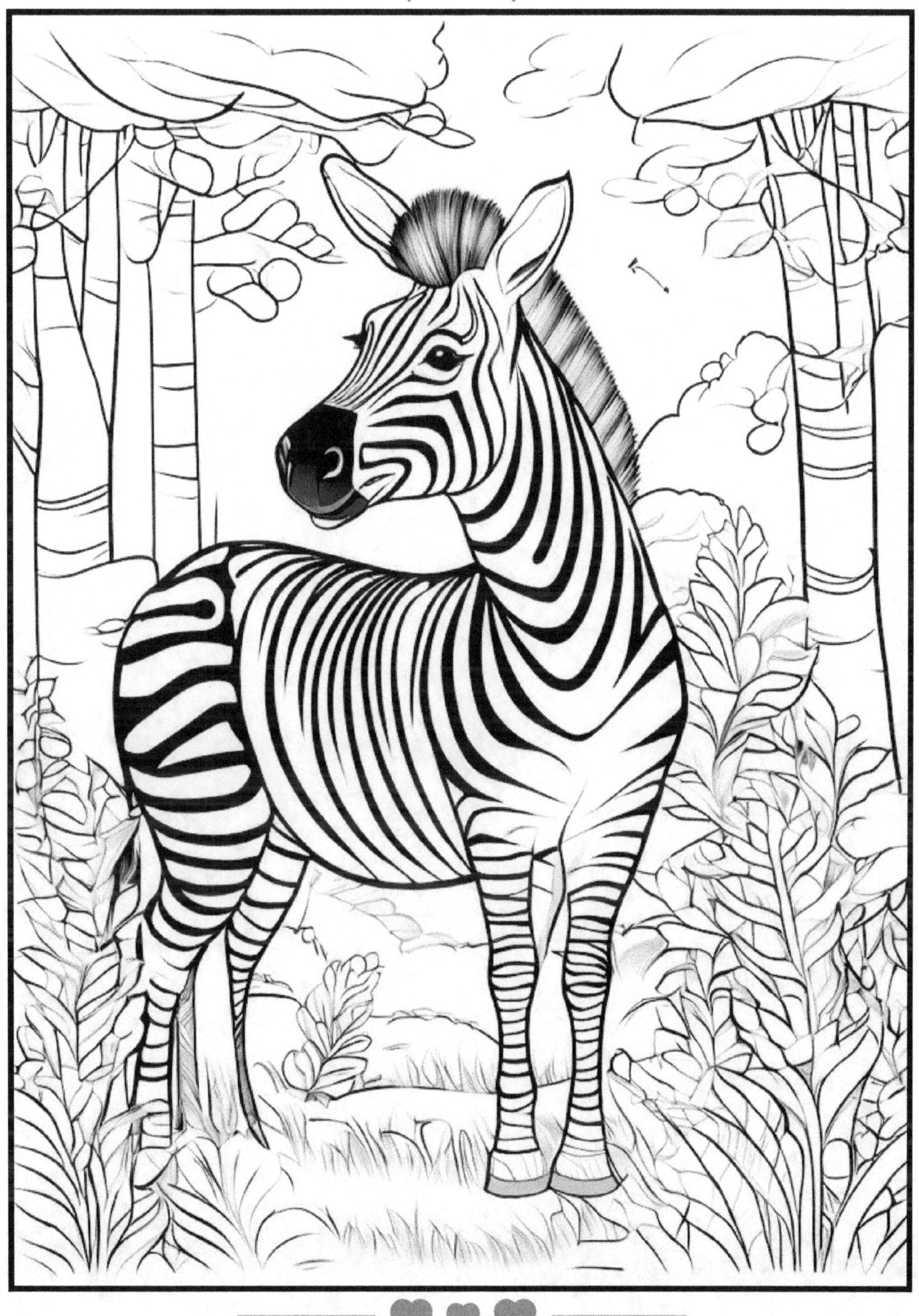

giraffe

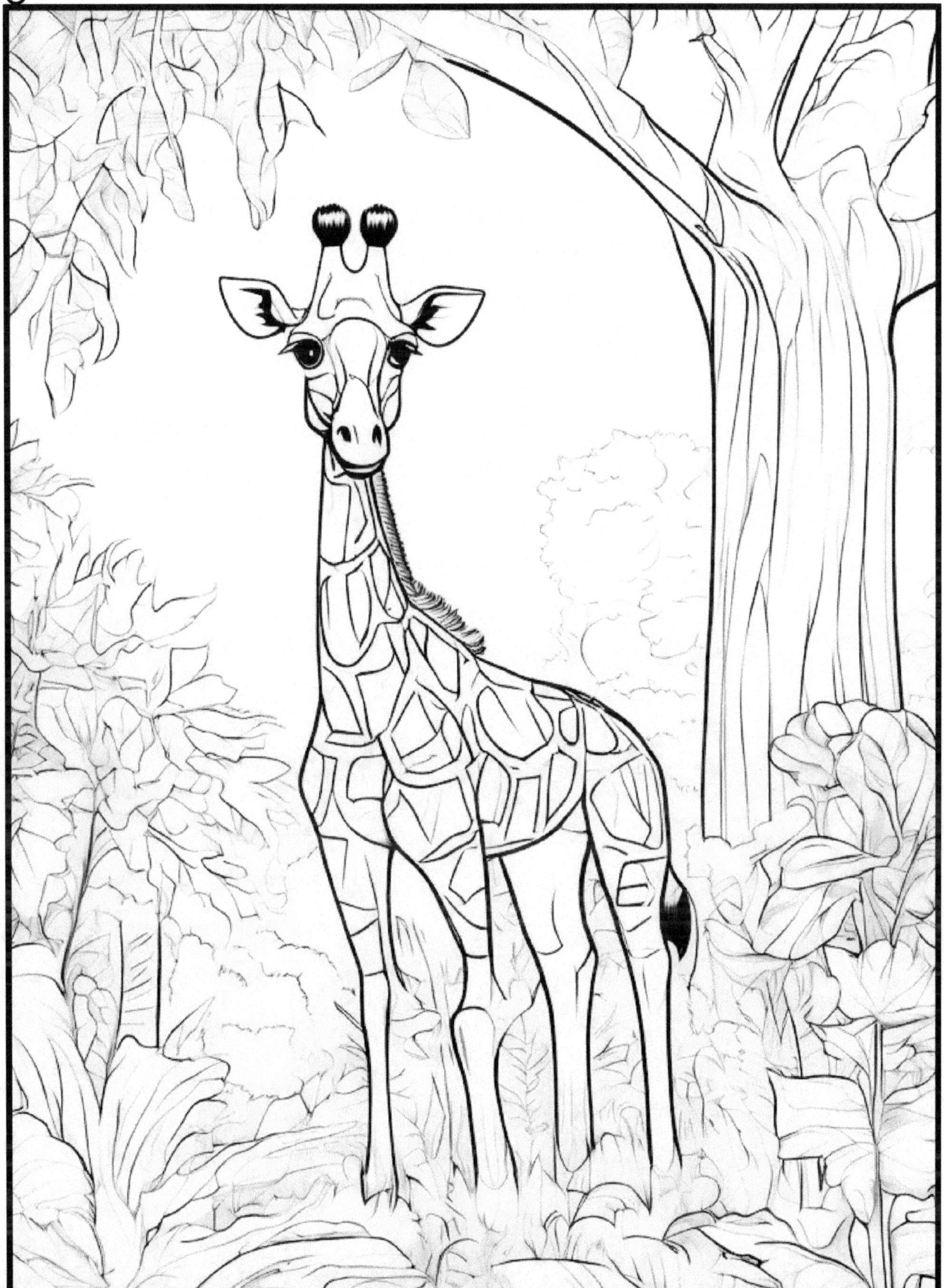

rhino

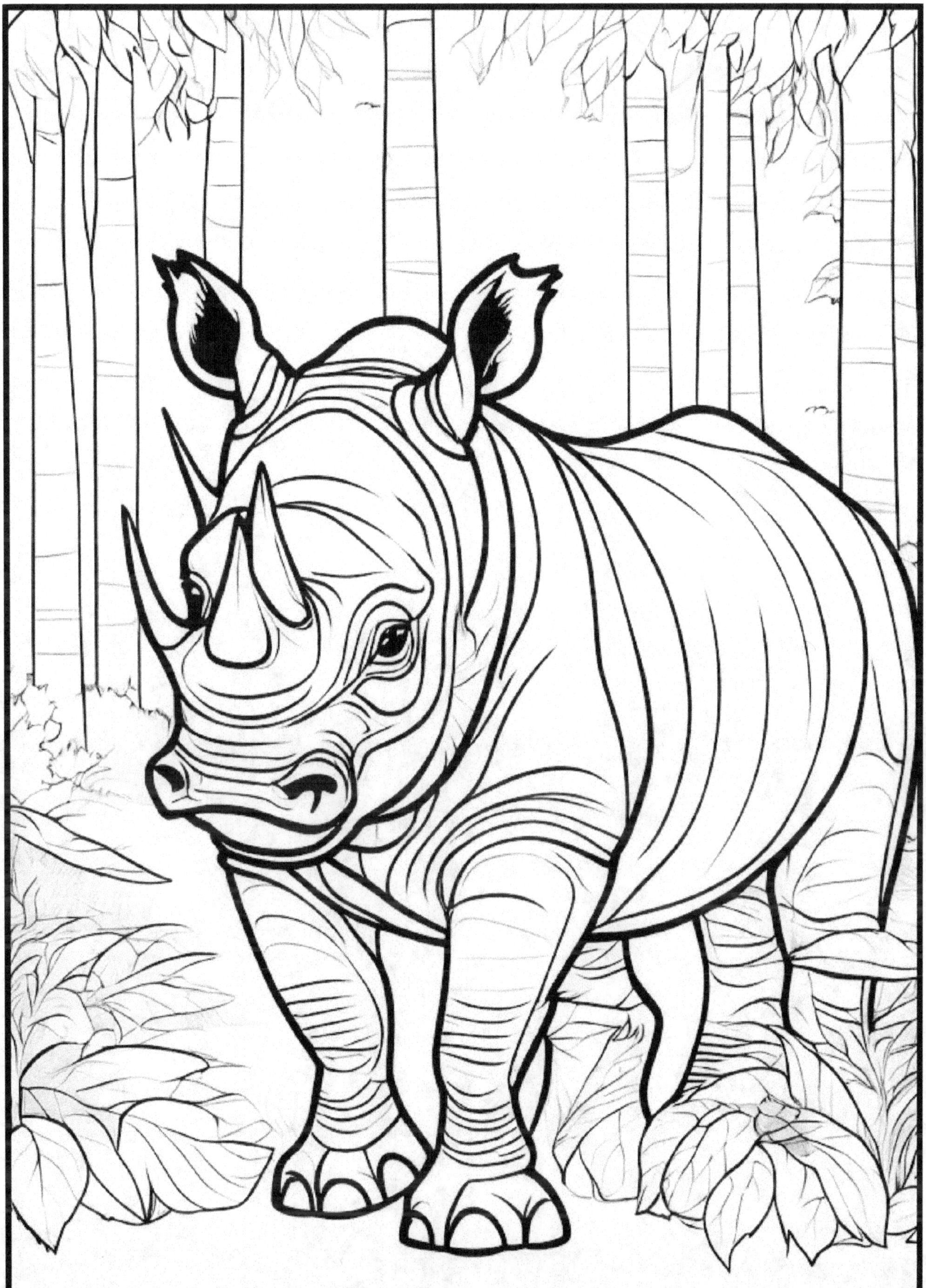

deer

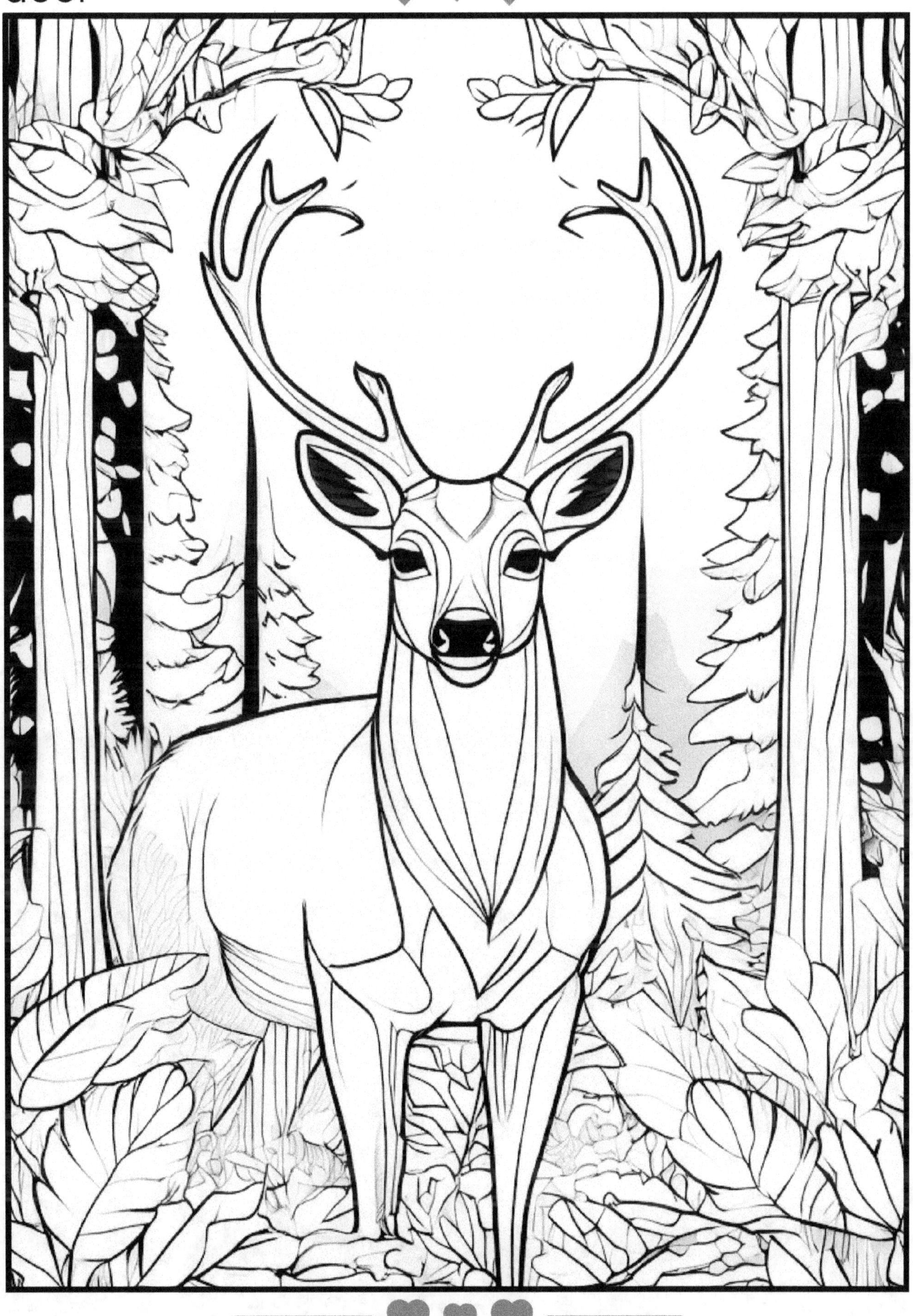

frog

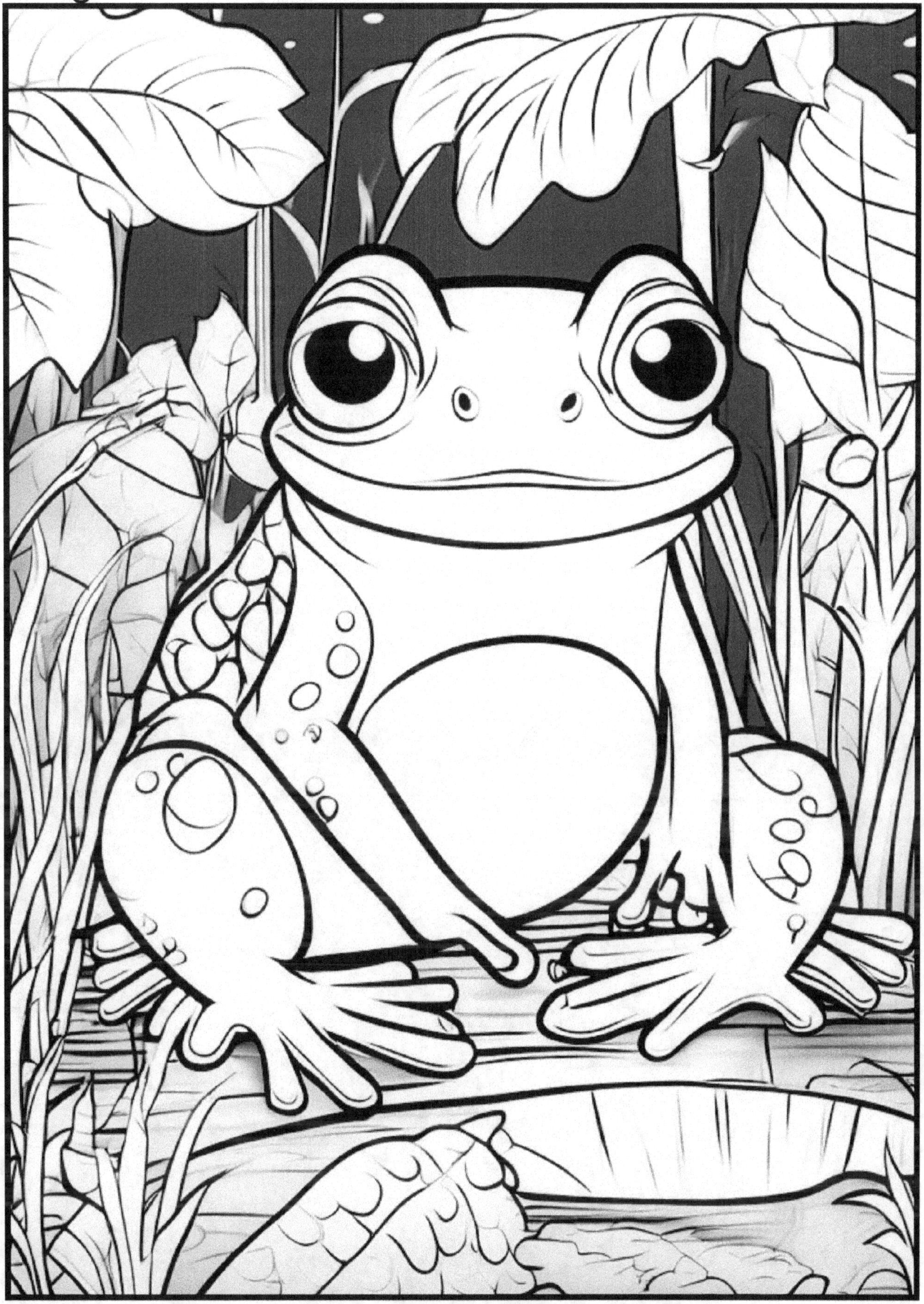

leopard

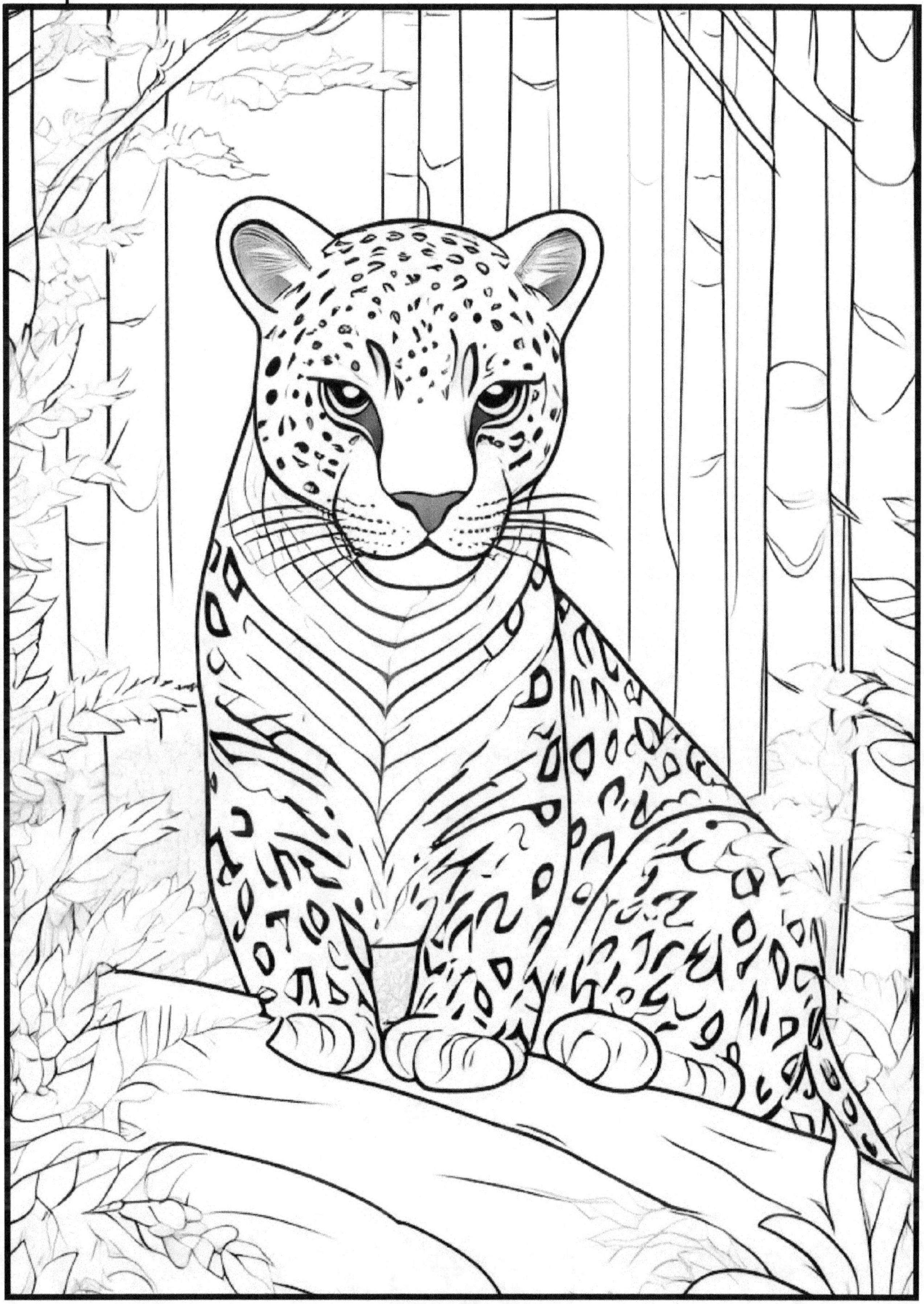

Hyena

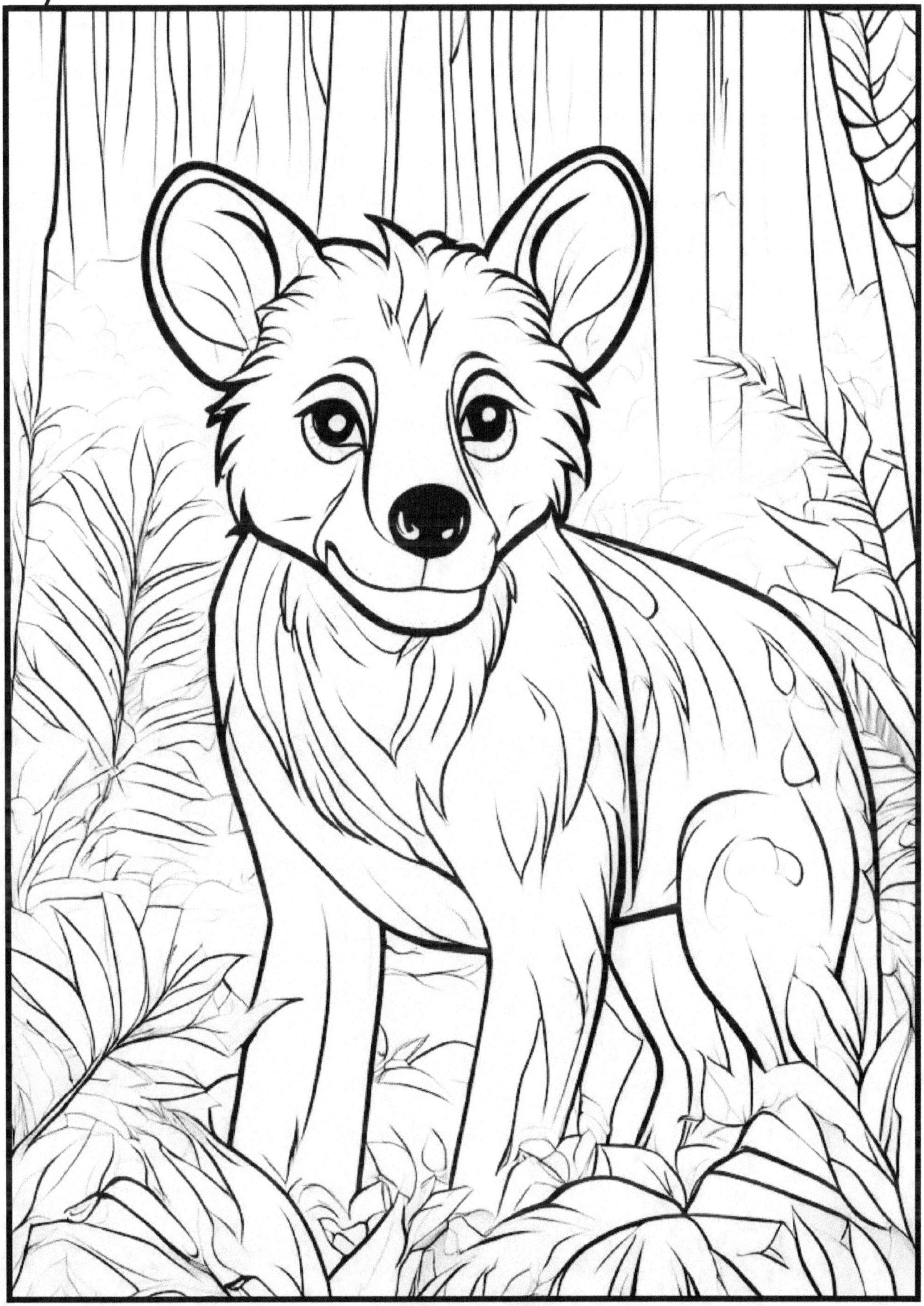

Buffalo

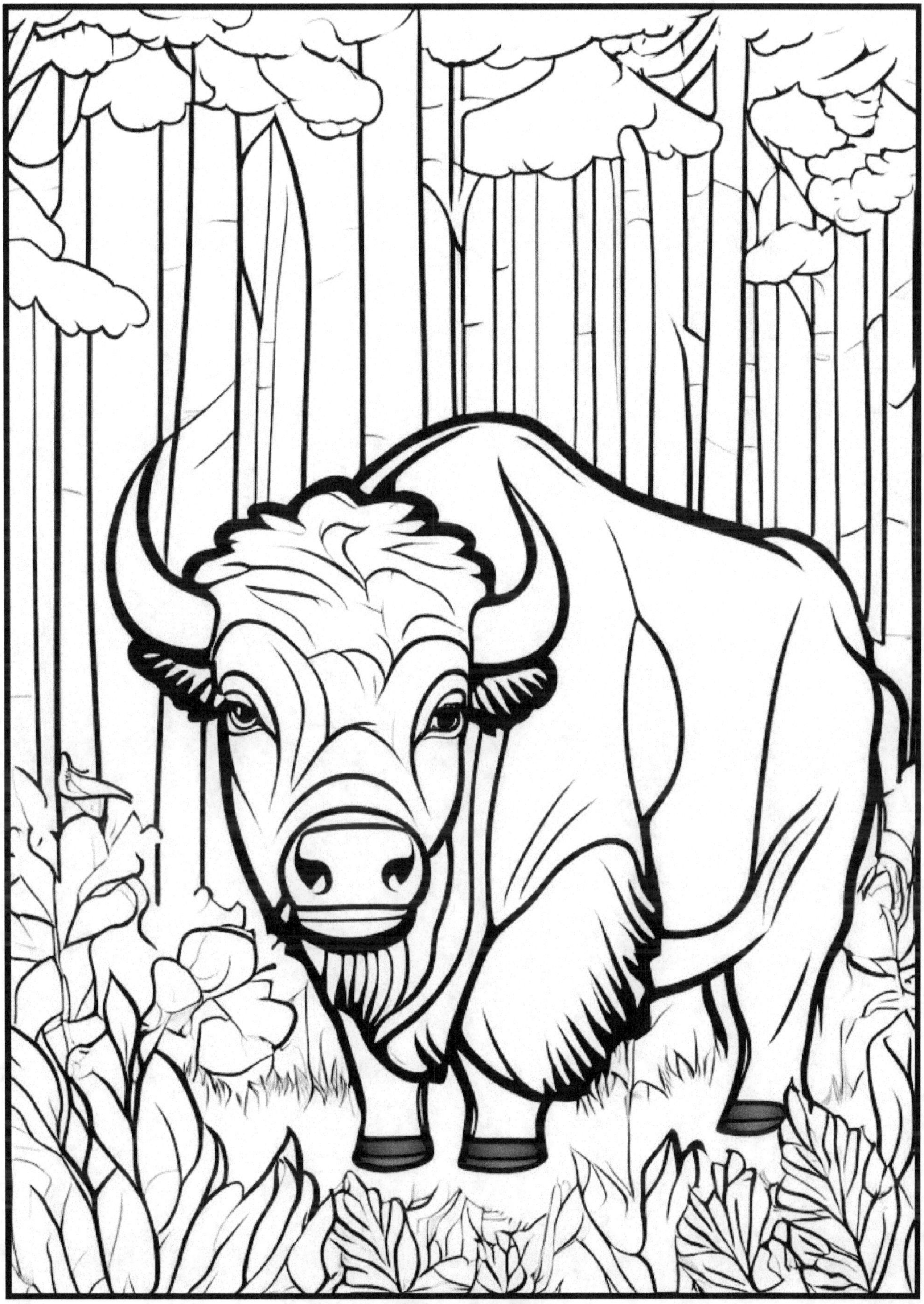

Crocodile

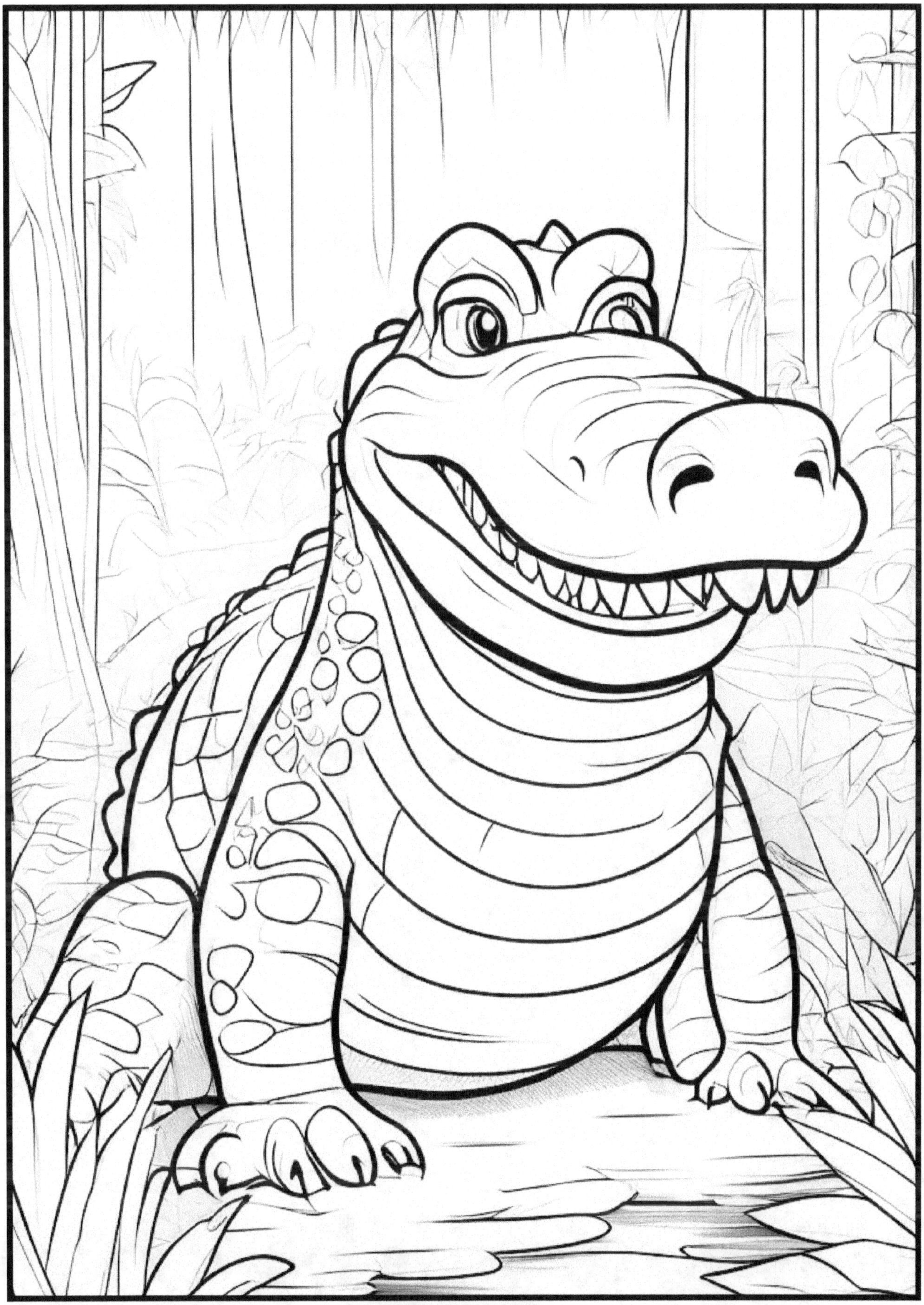

Ostrich

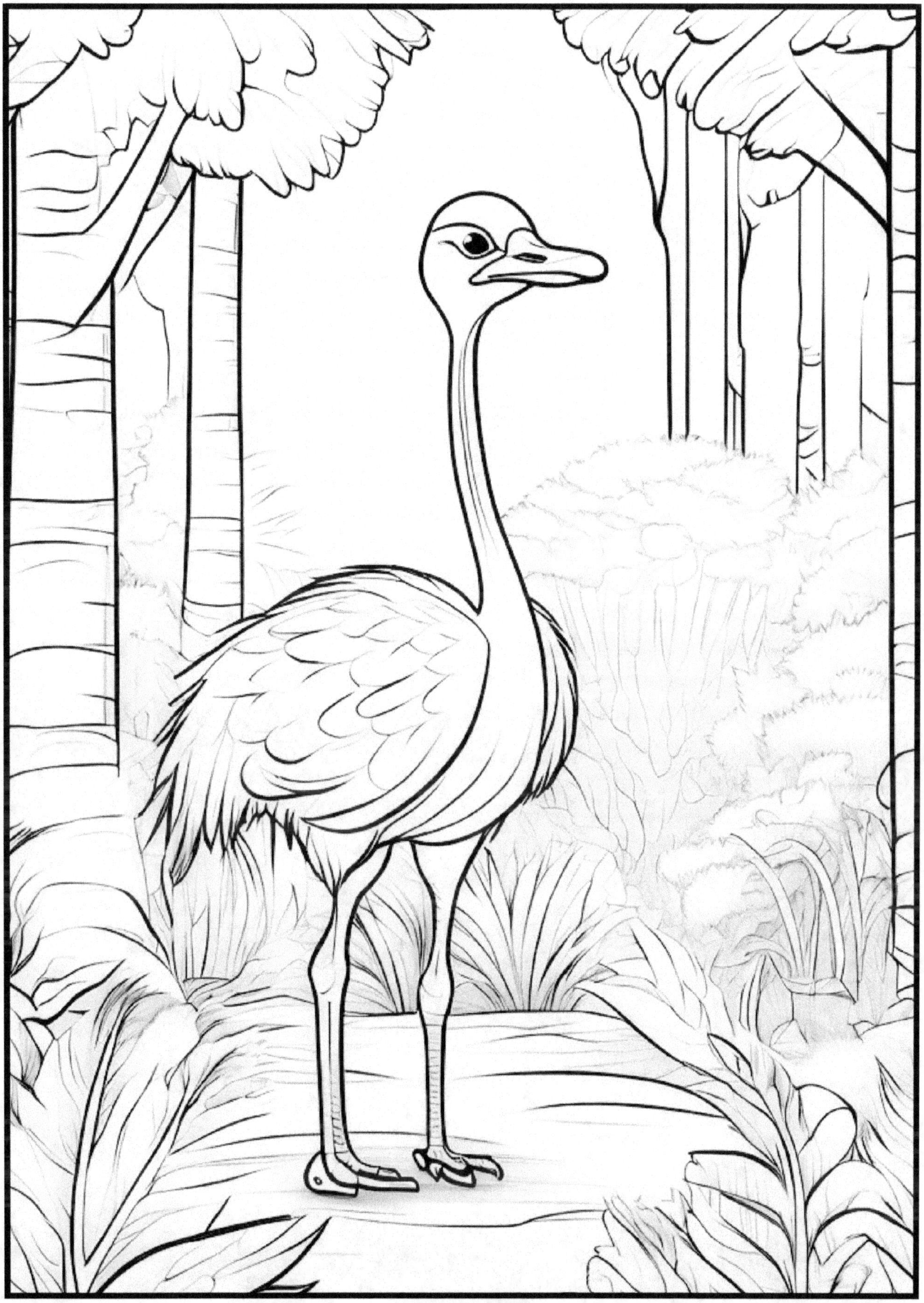

Atheris

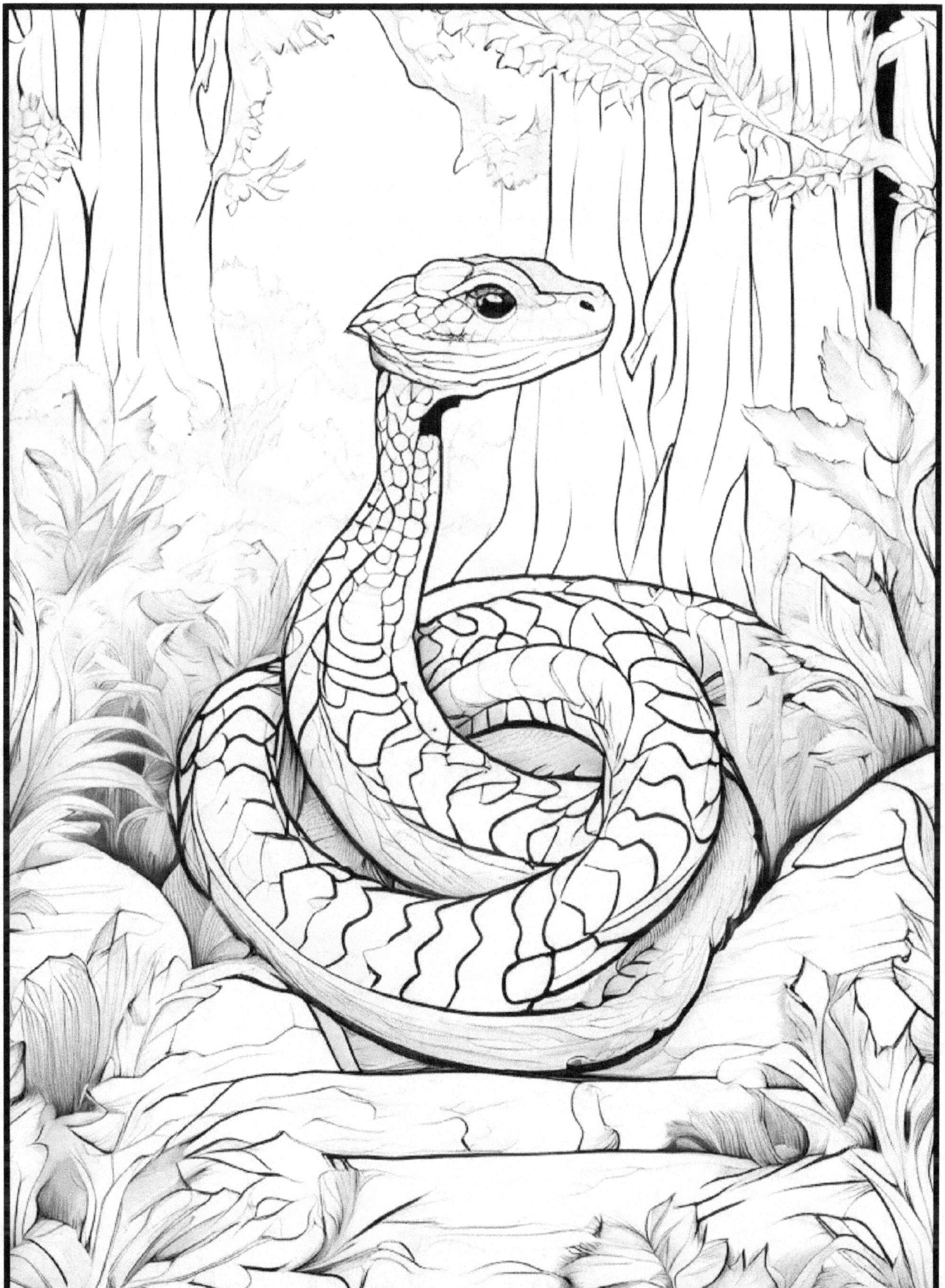

Meerkat

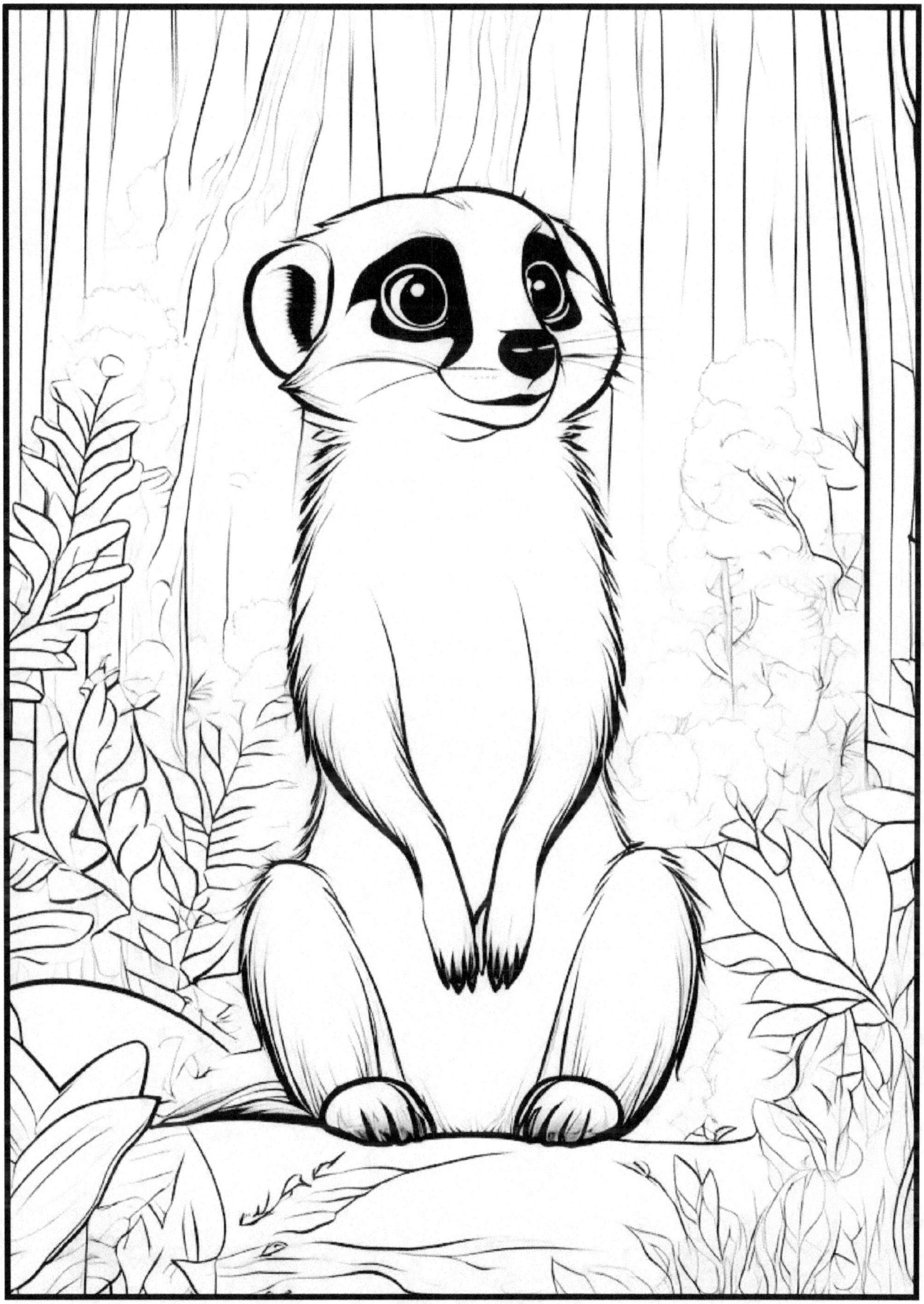

cheetah

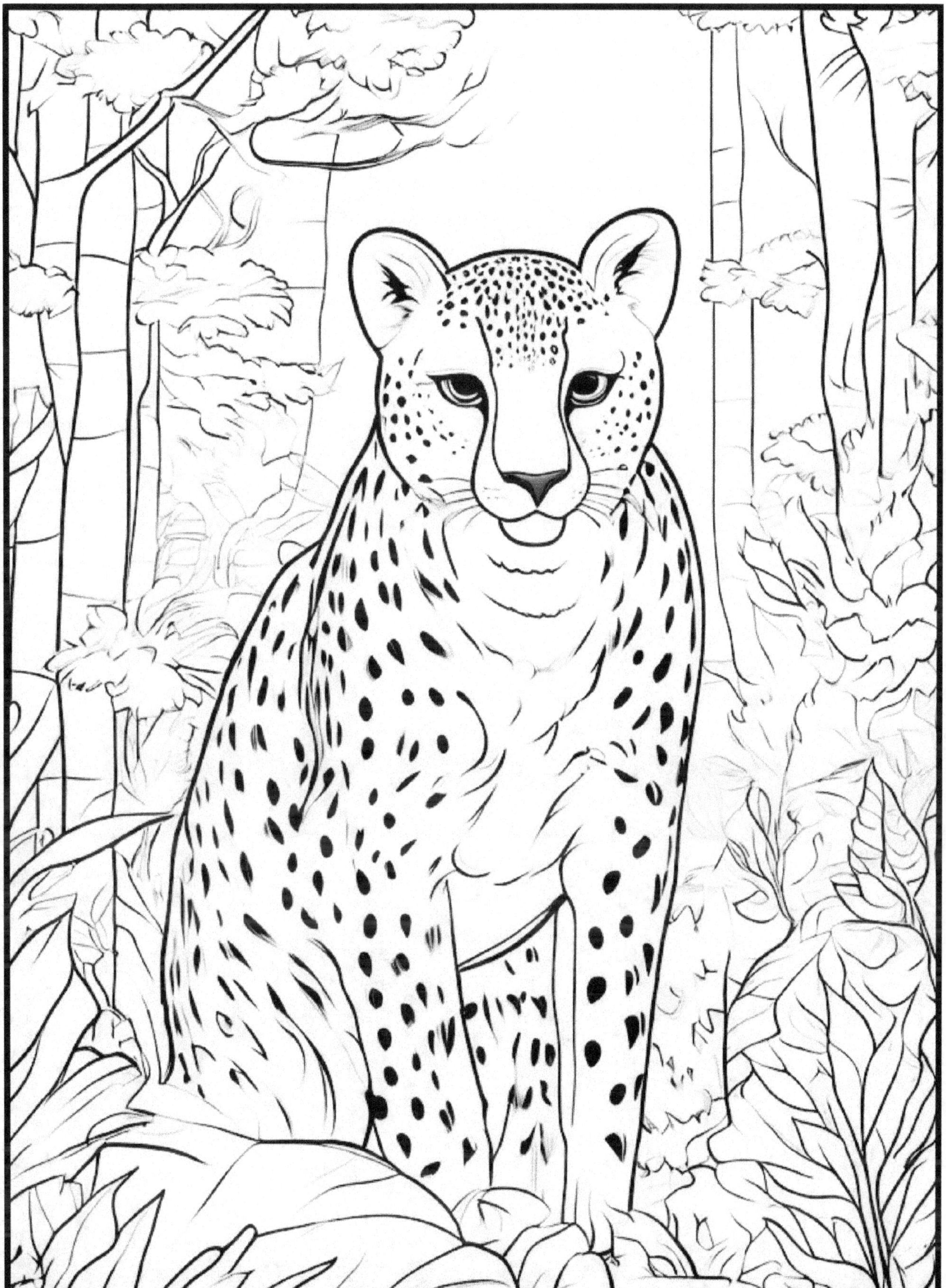

gorilla

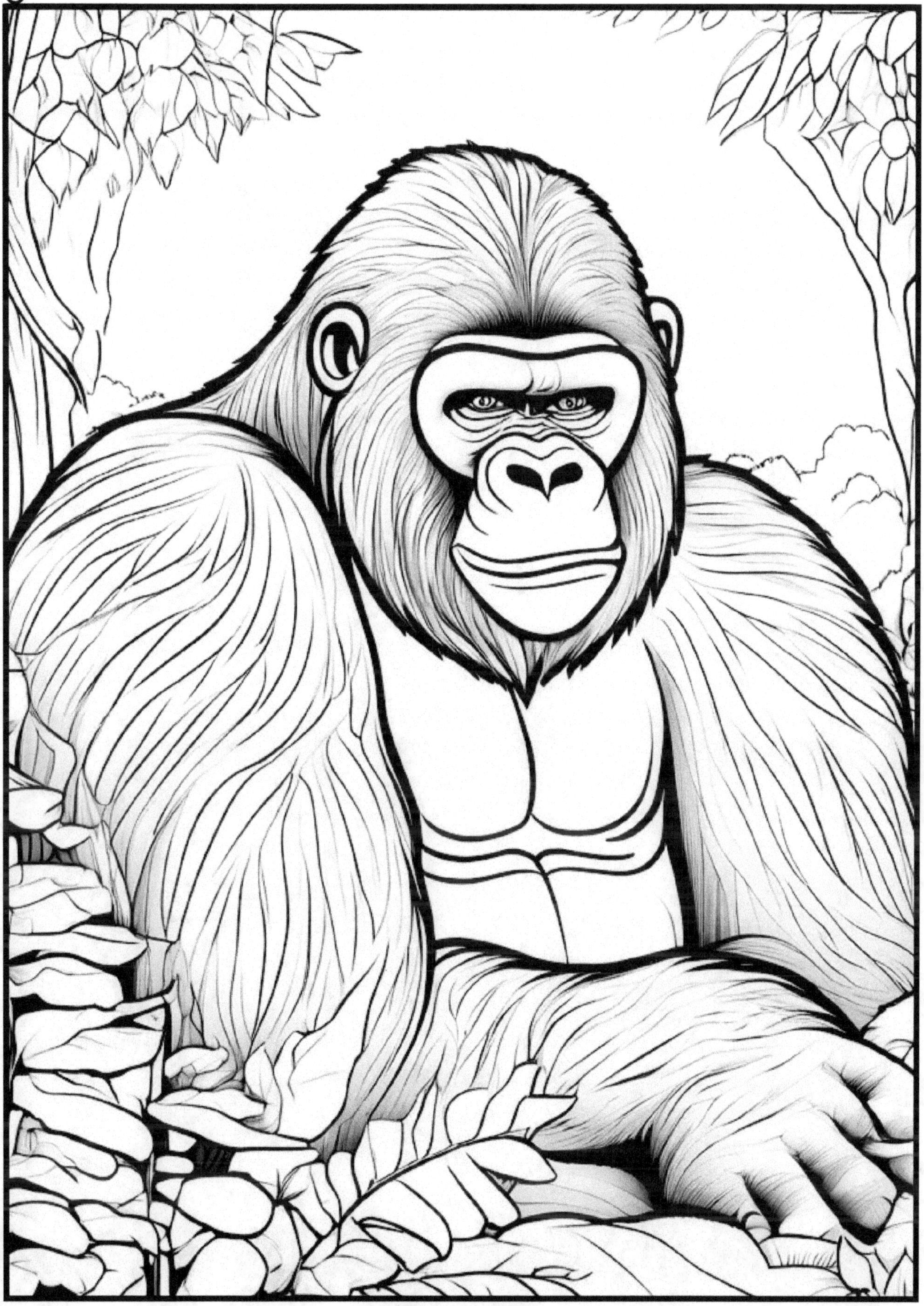

gnu

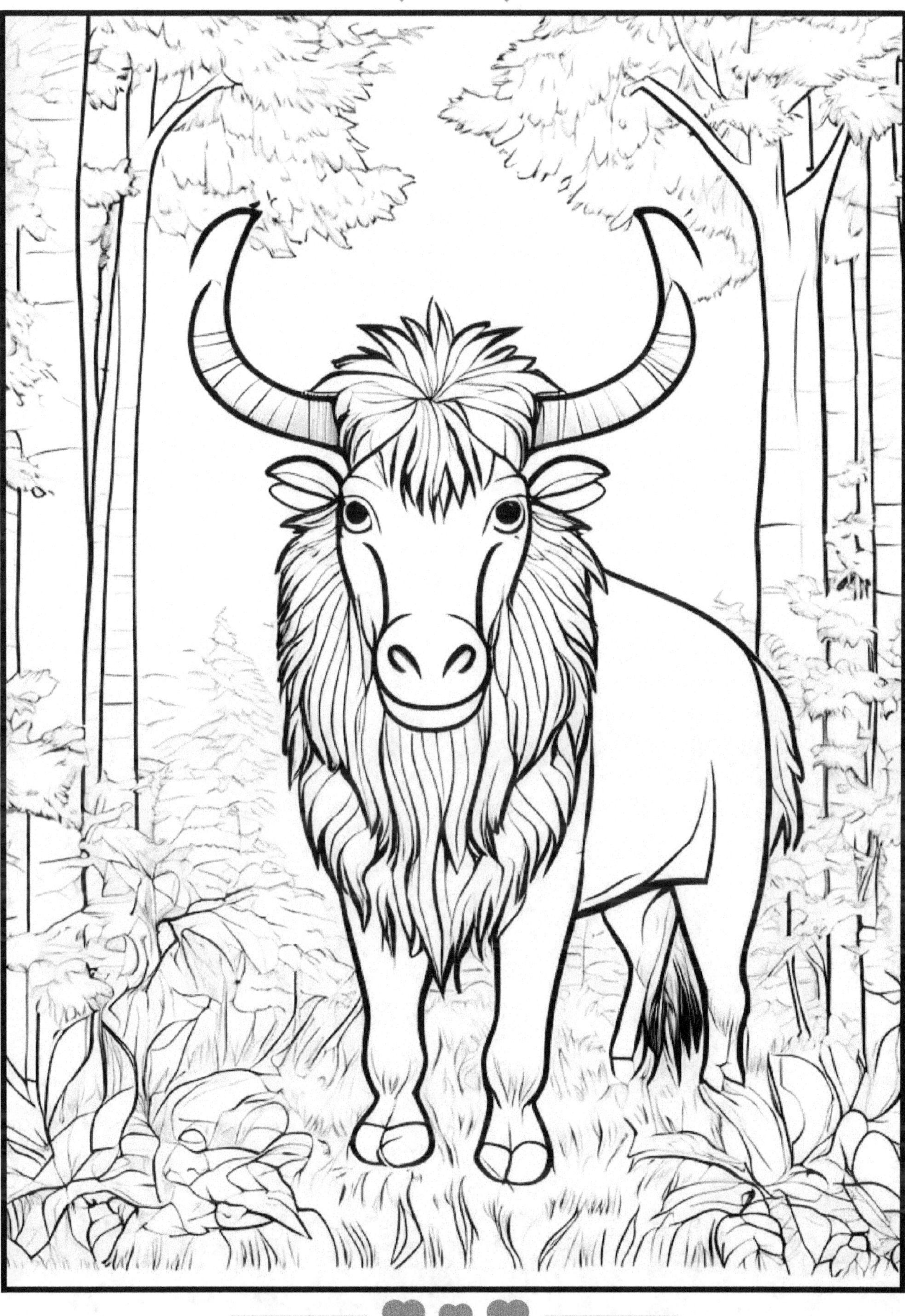

Locust

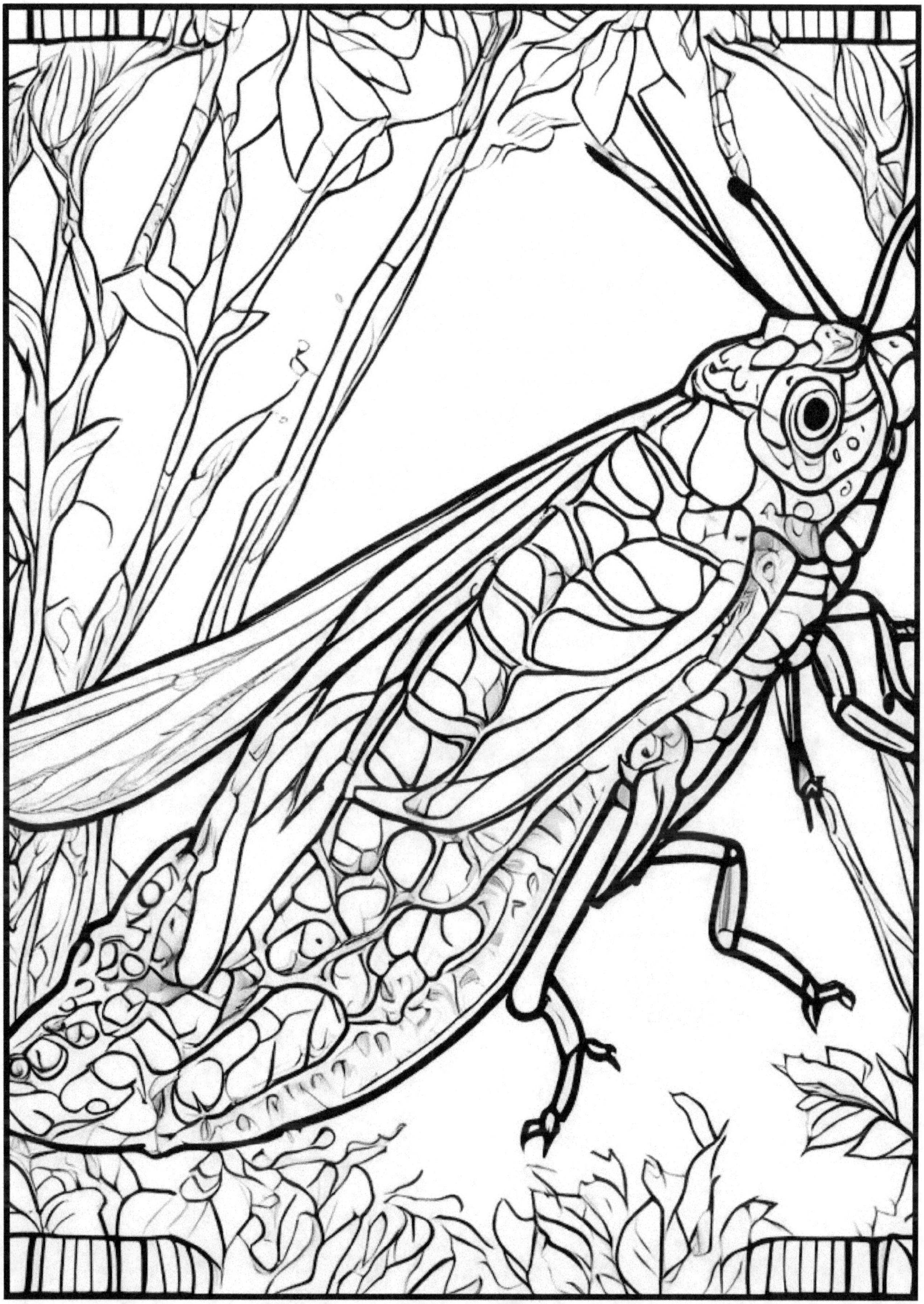

boar

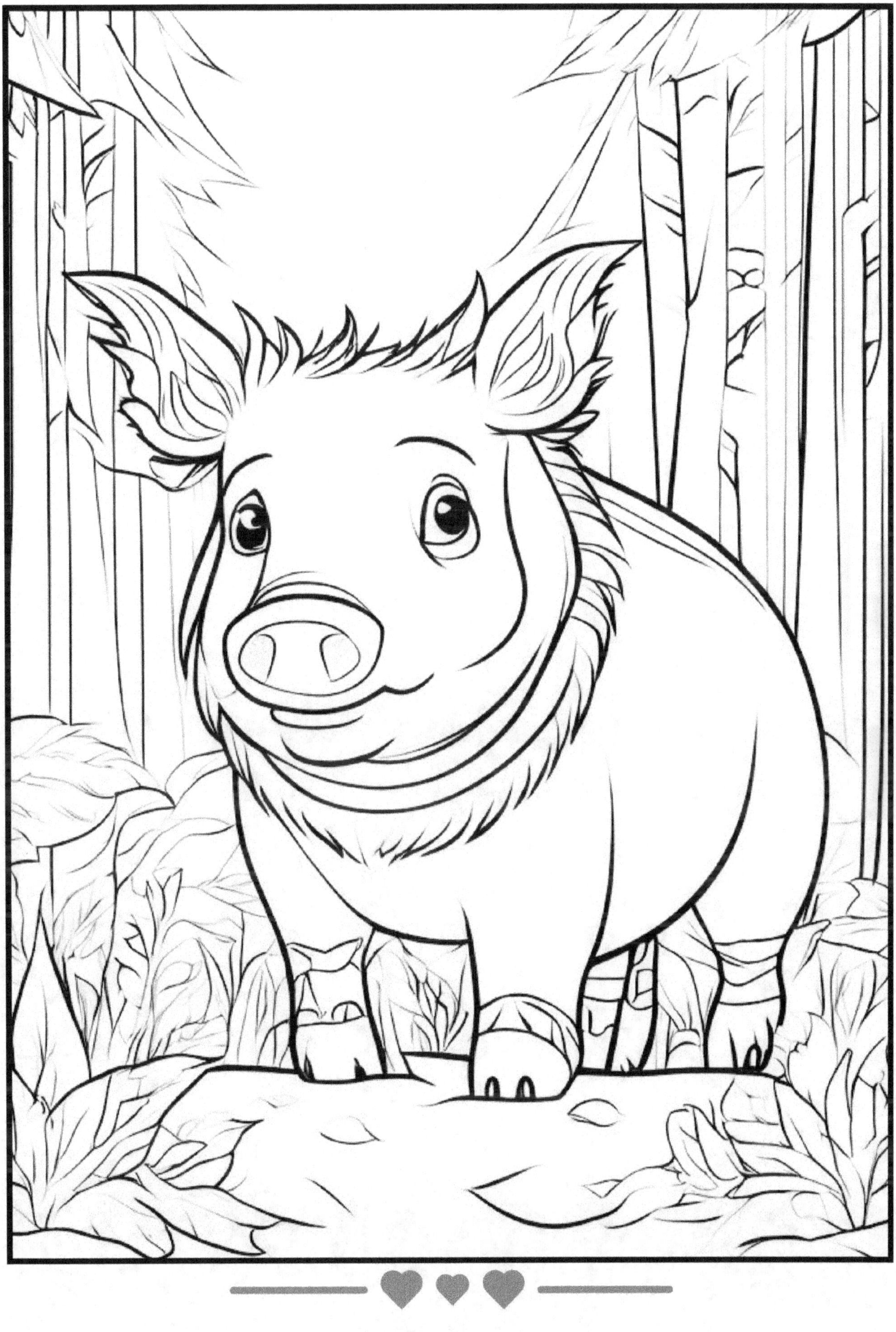

Wolf

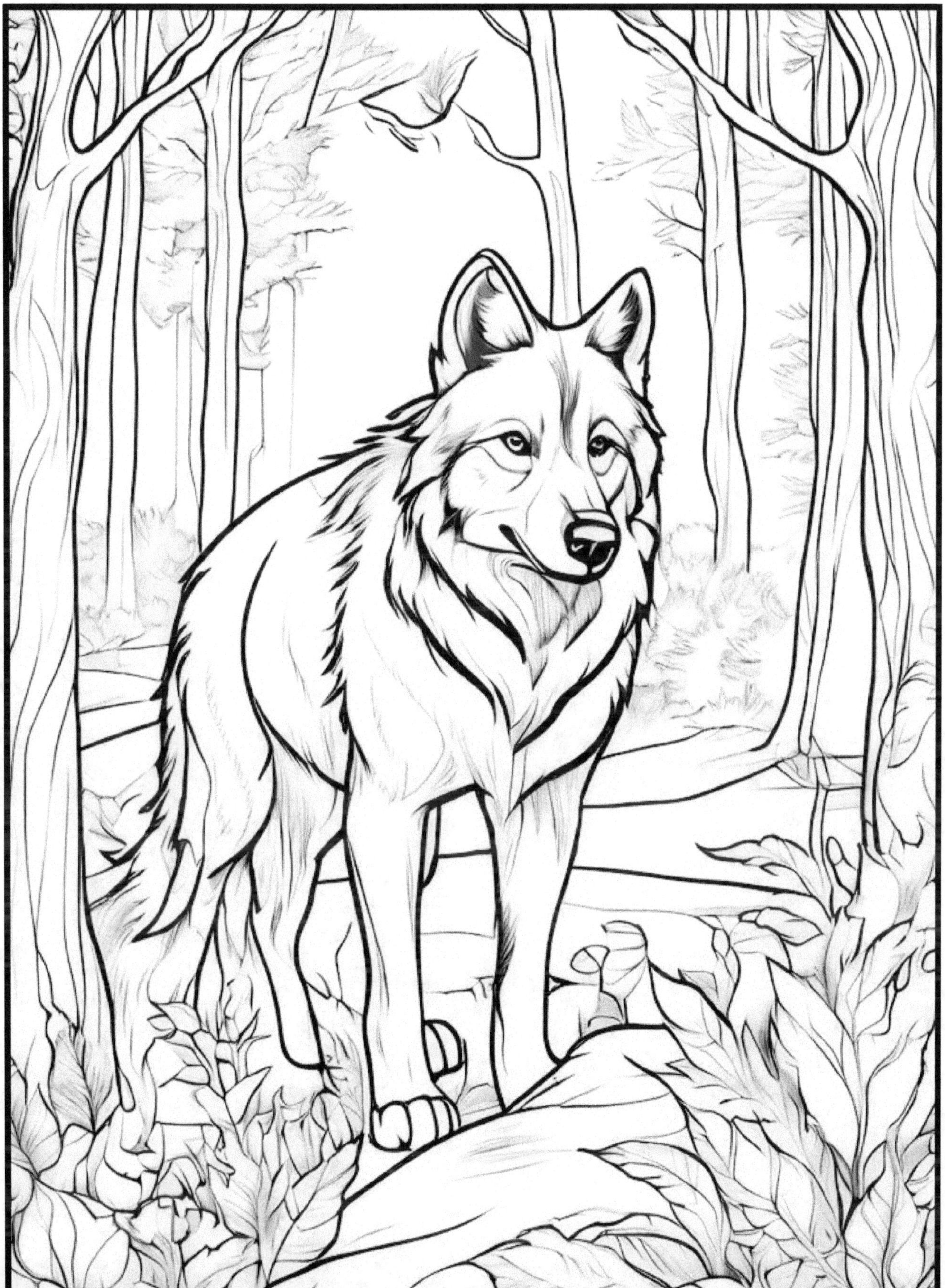

unicorn

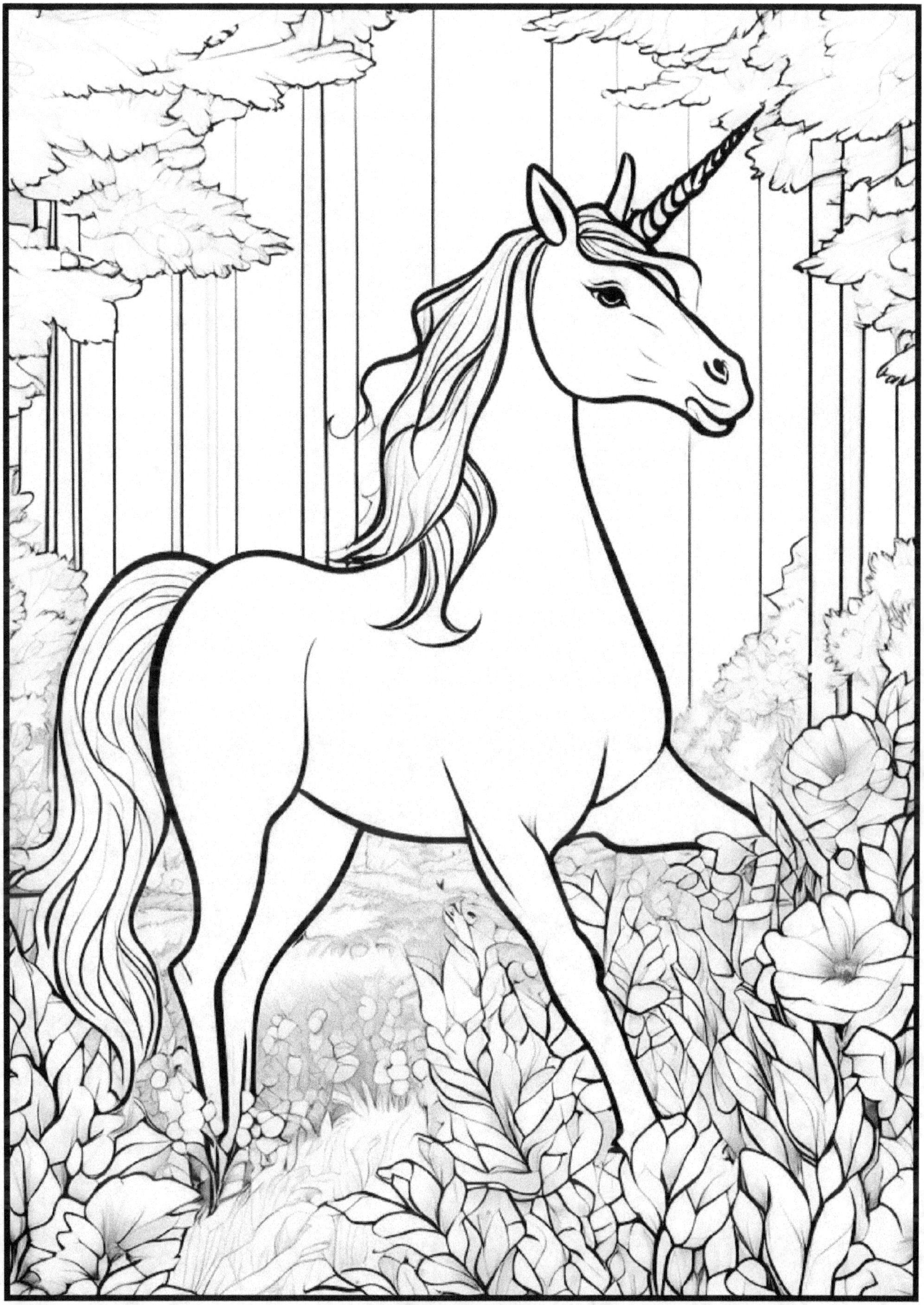

parrot

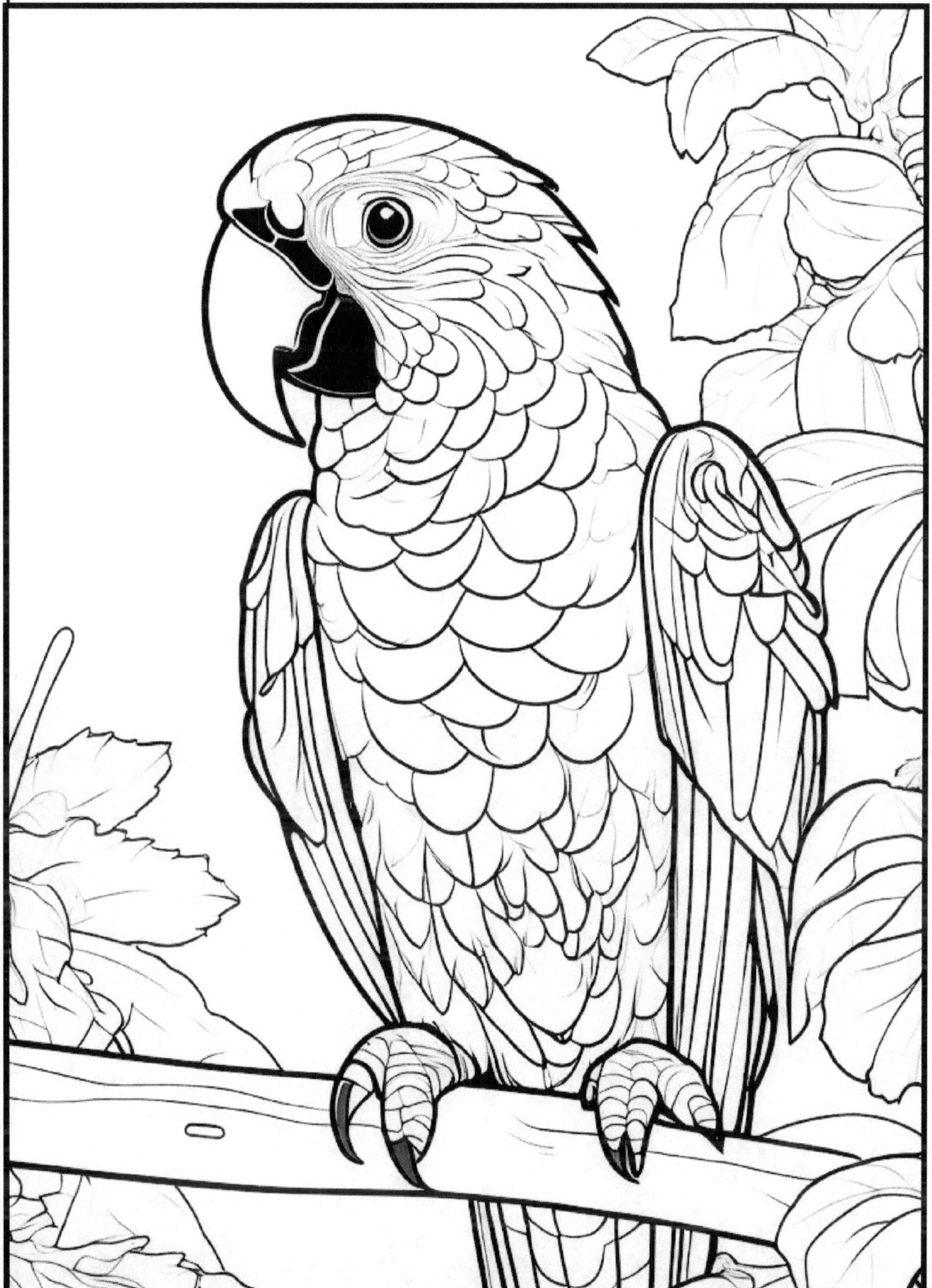

Crow-crowned

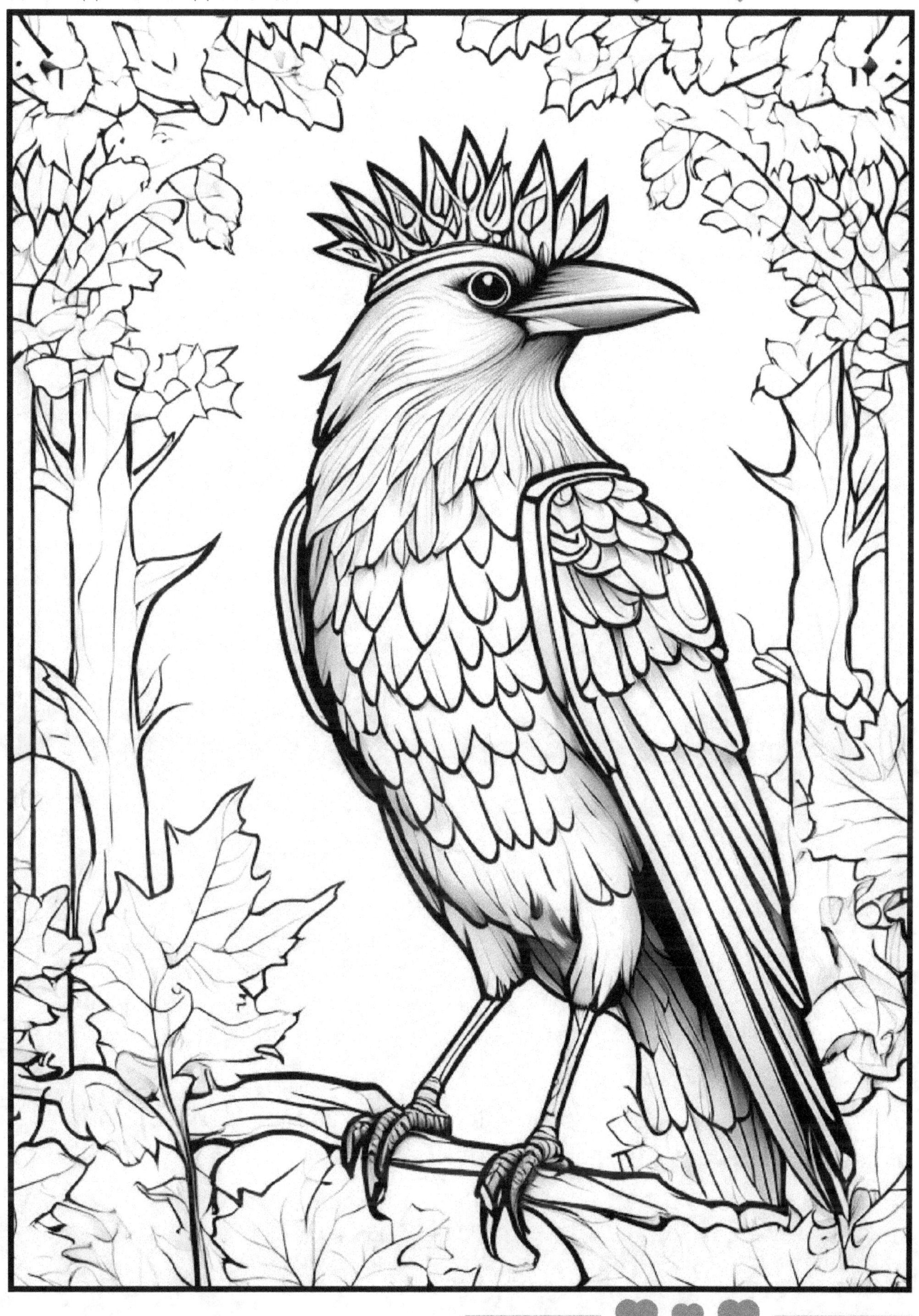

turtle

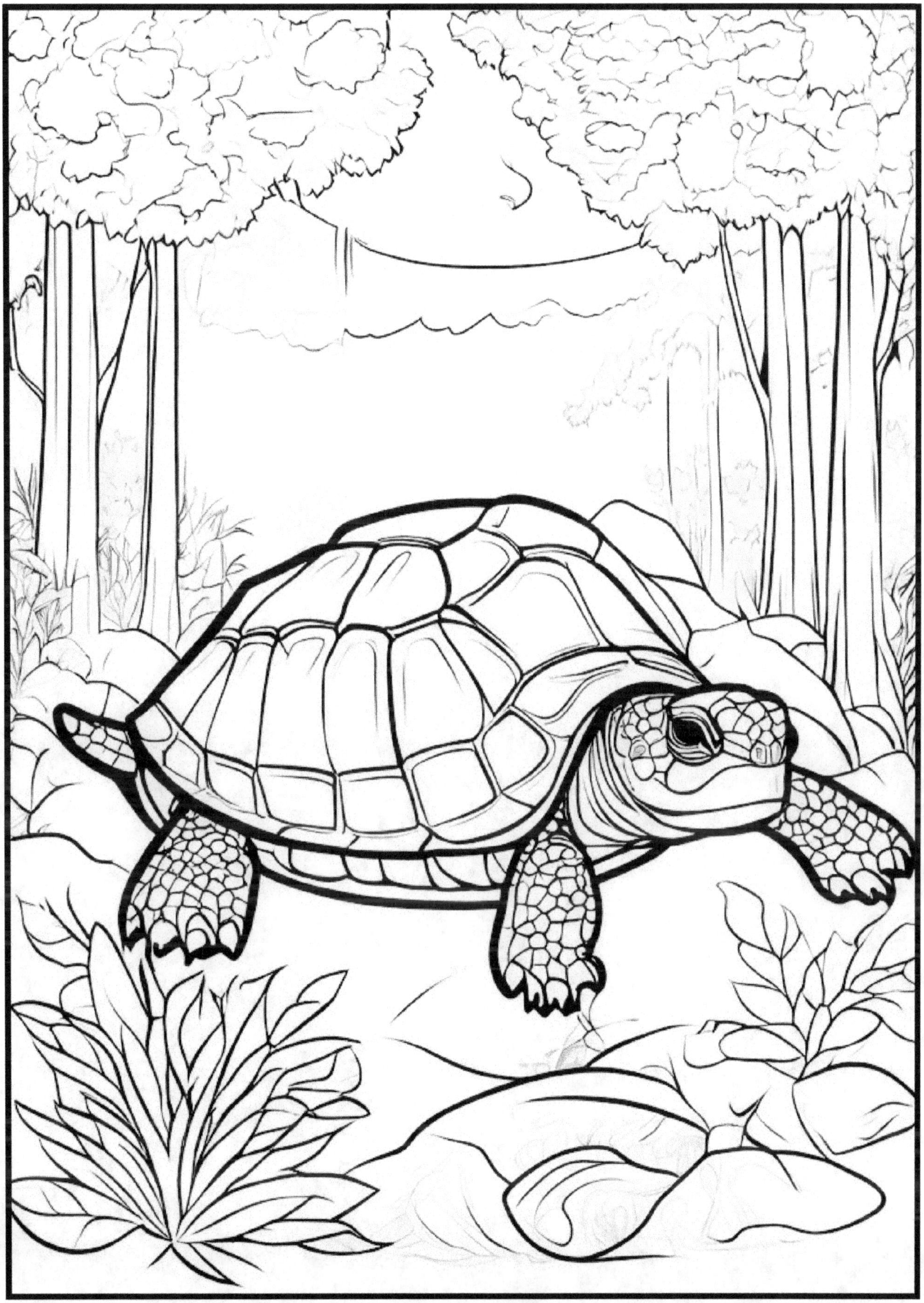

eagle

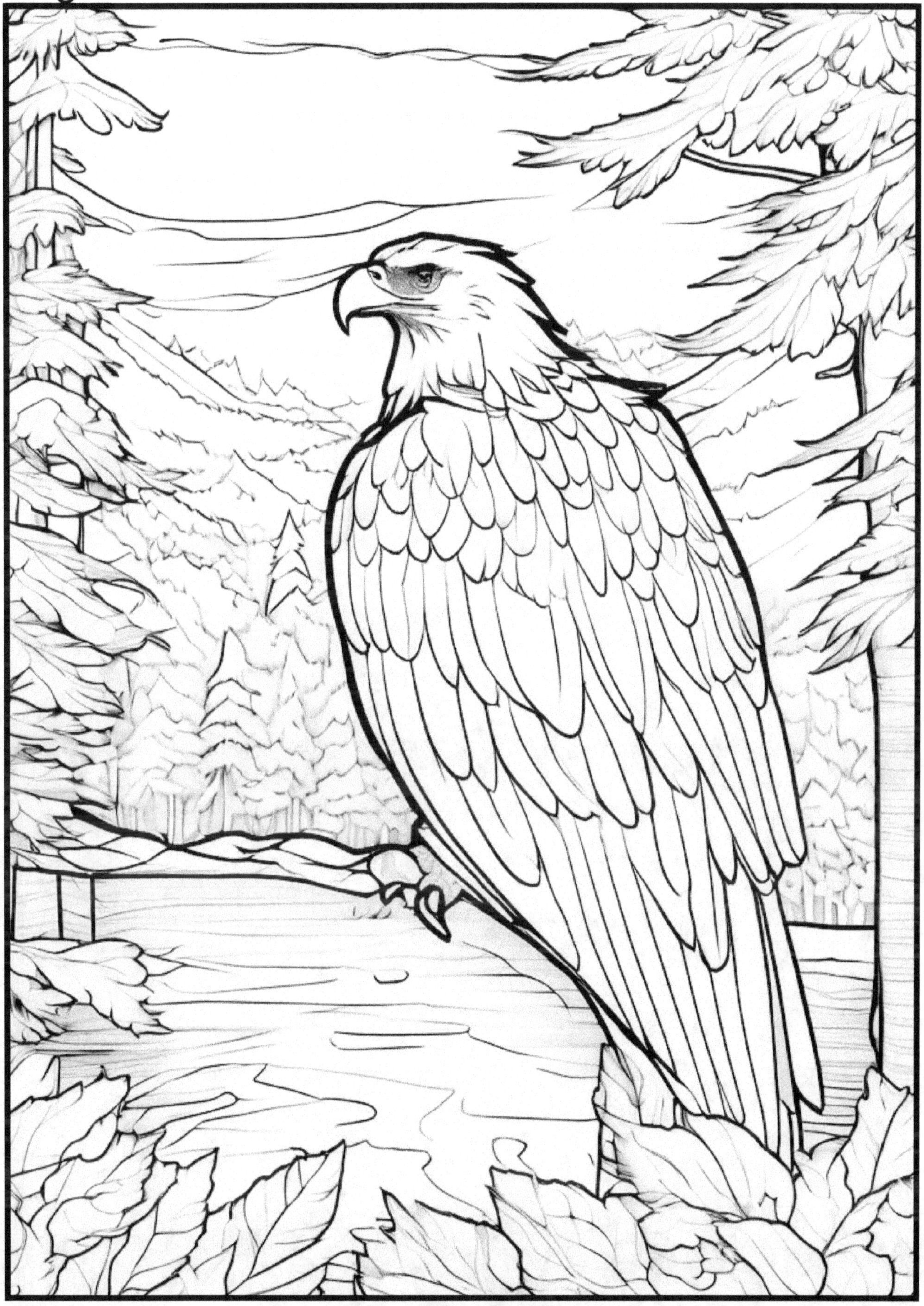

eagle

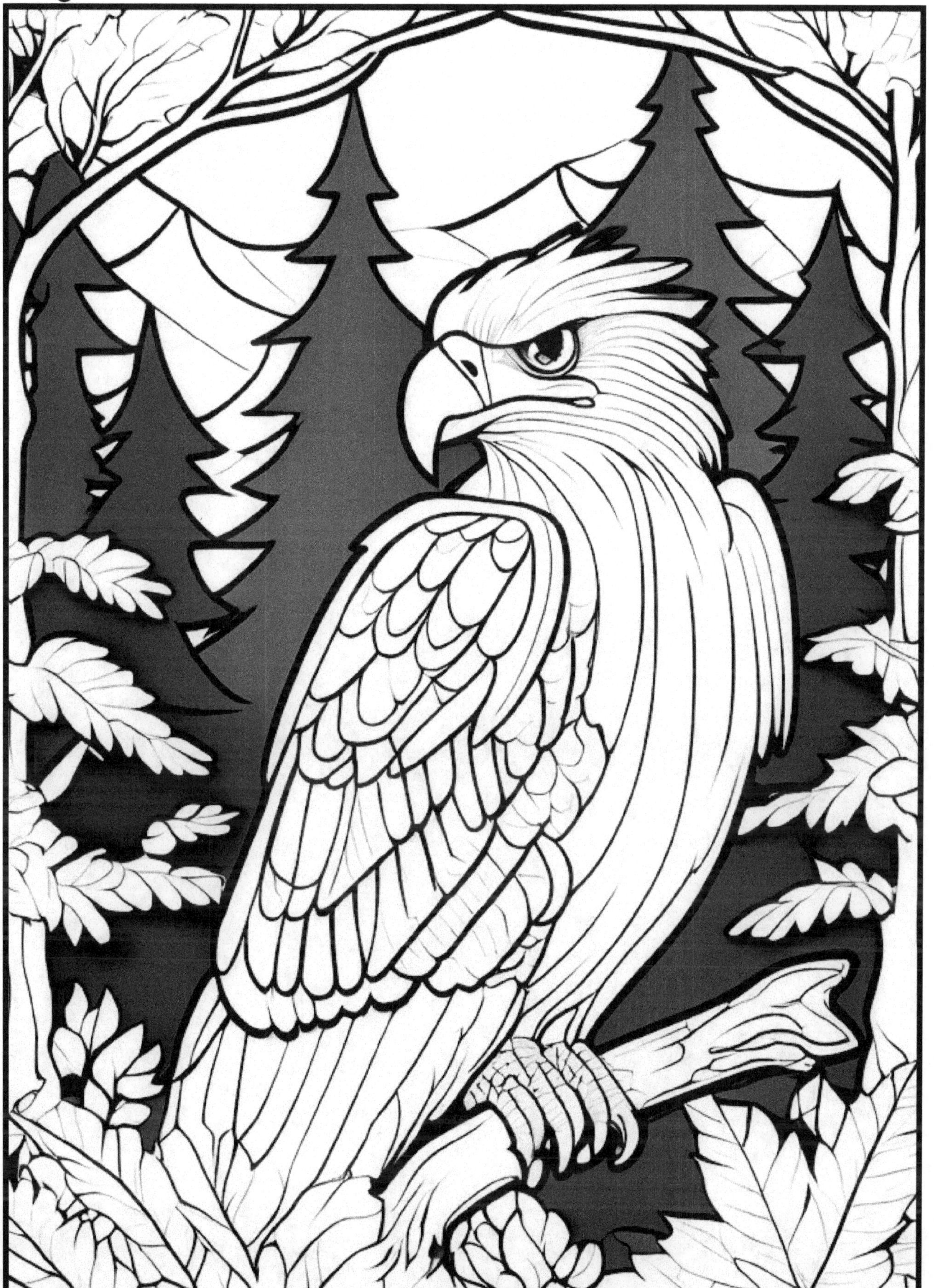

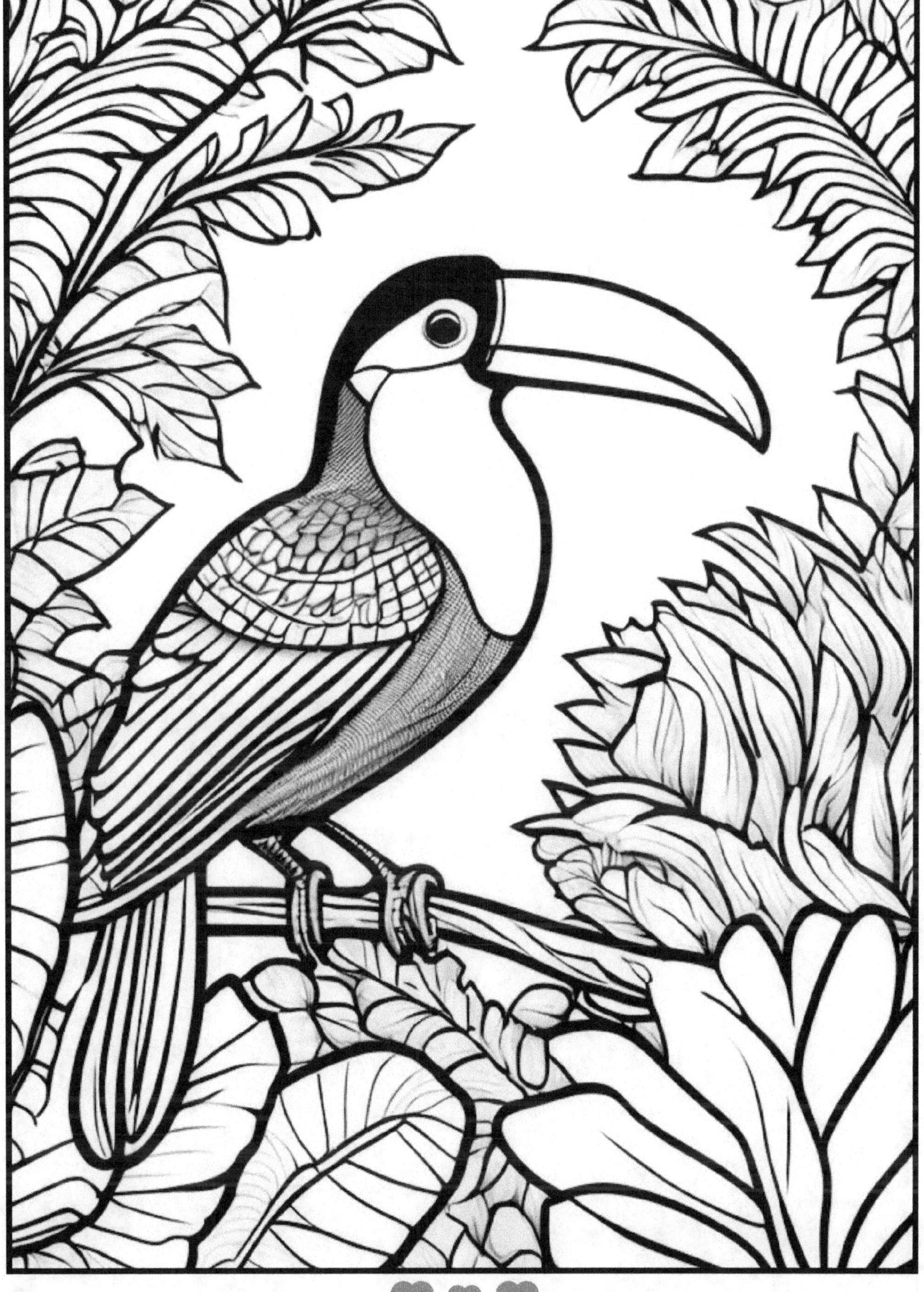
toucan

fox

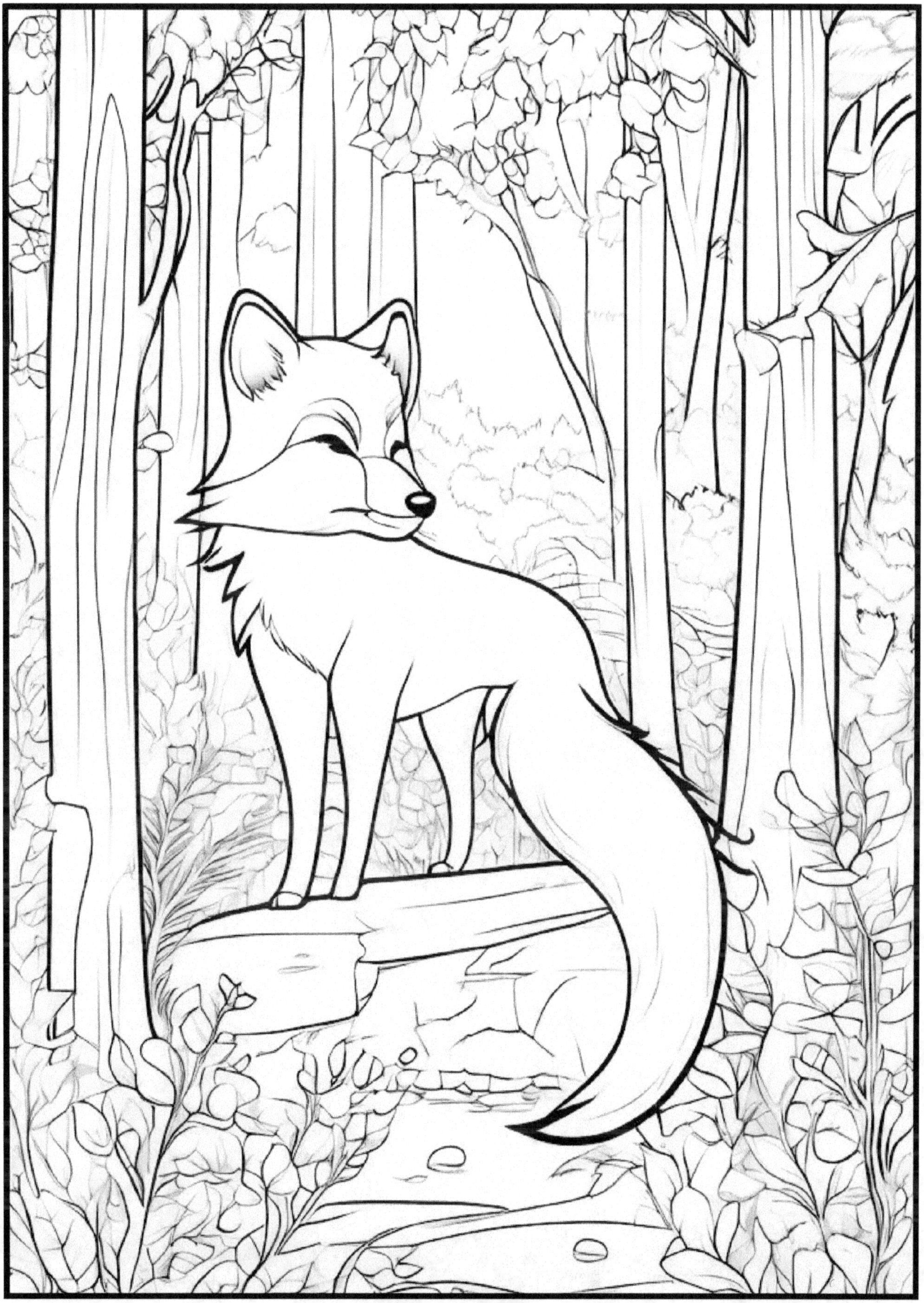

spider

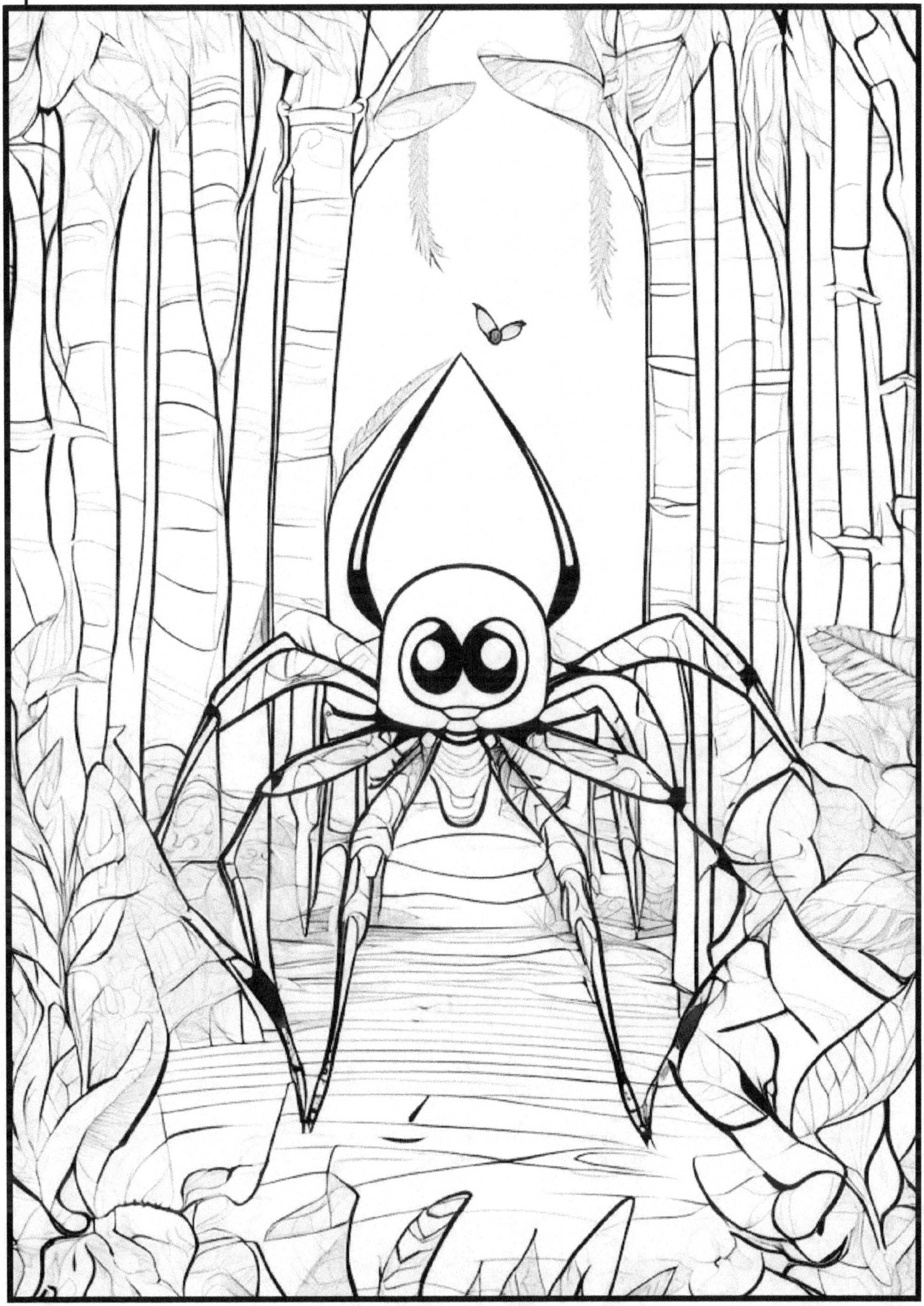

Panda bear

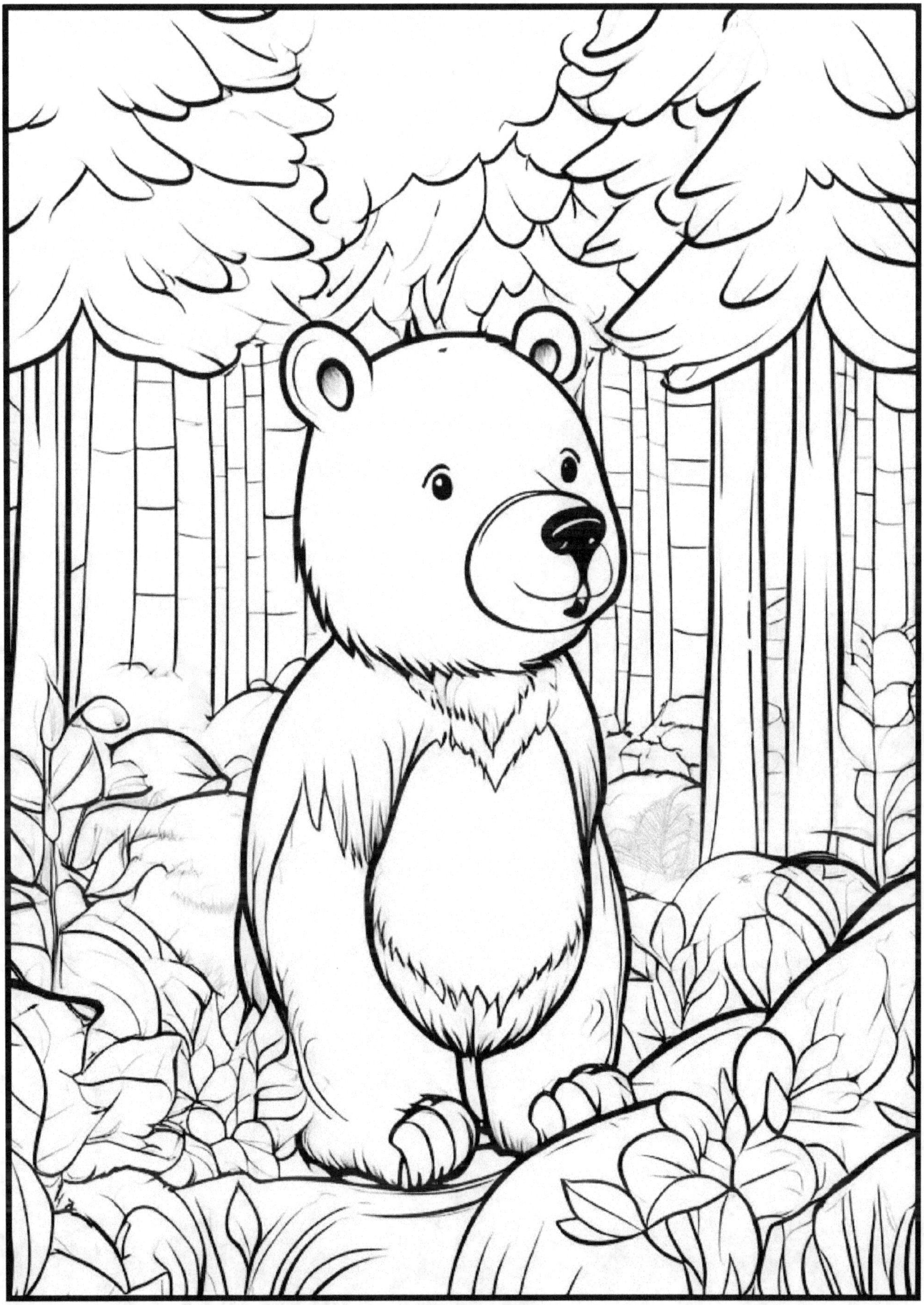

squirrel

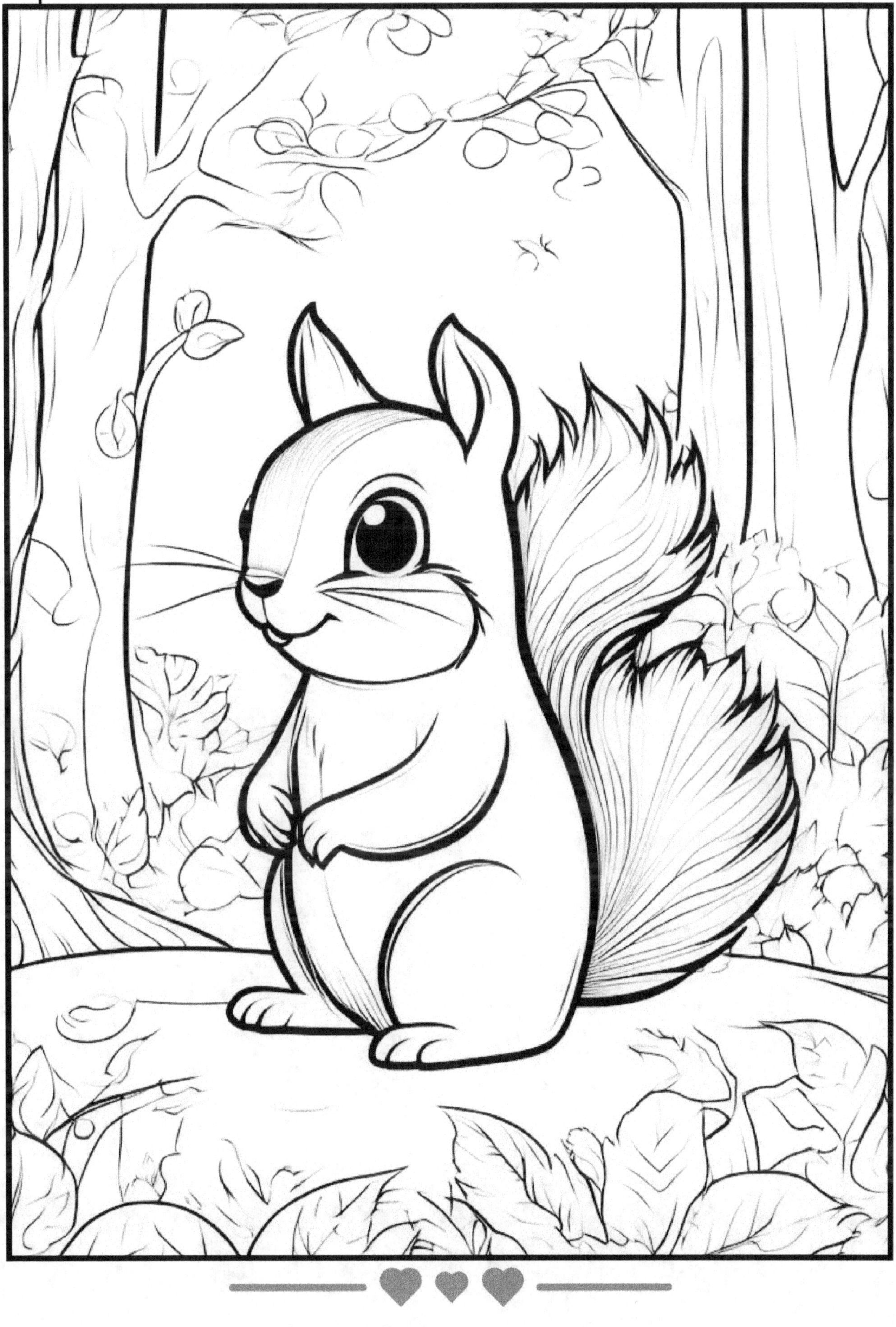

armadillo

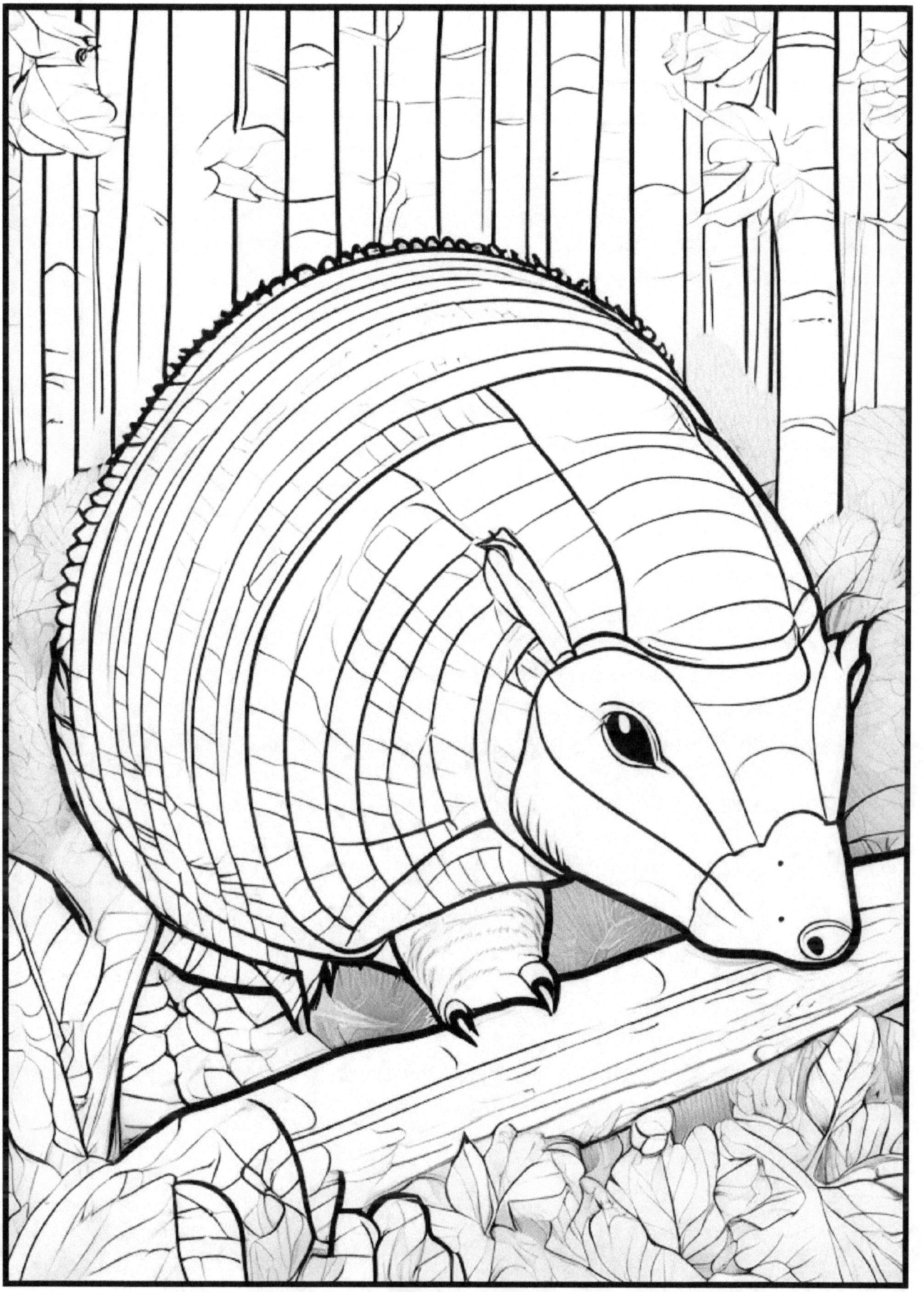

vulture

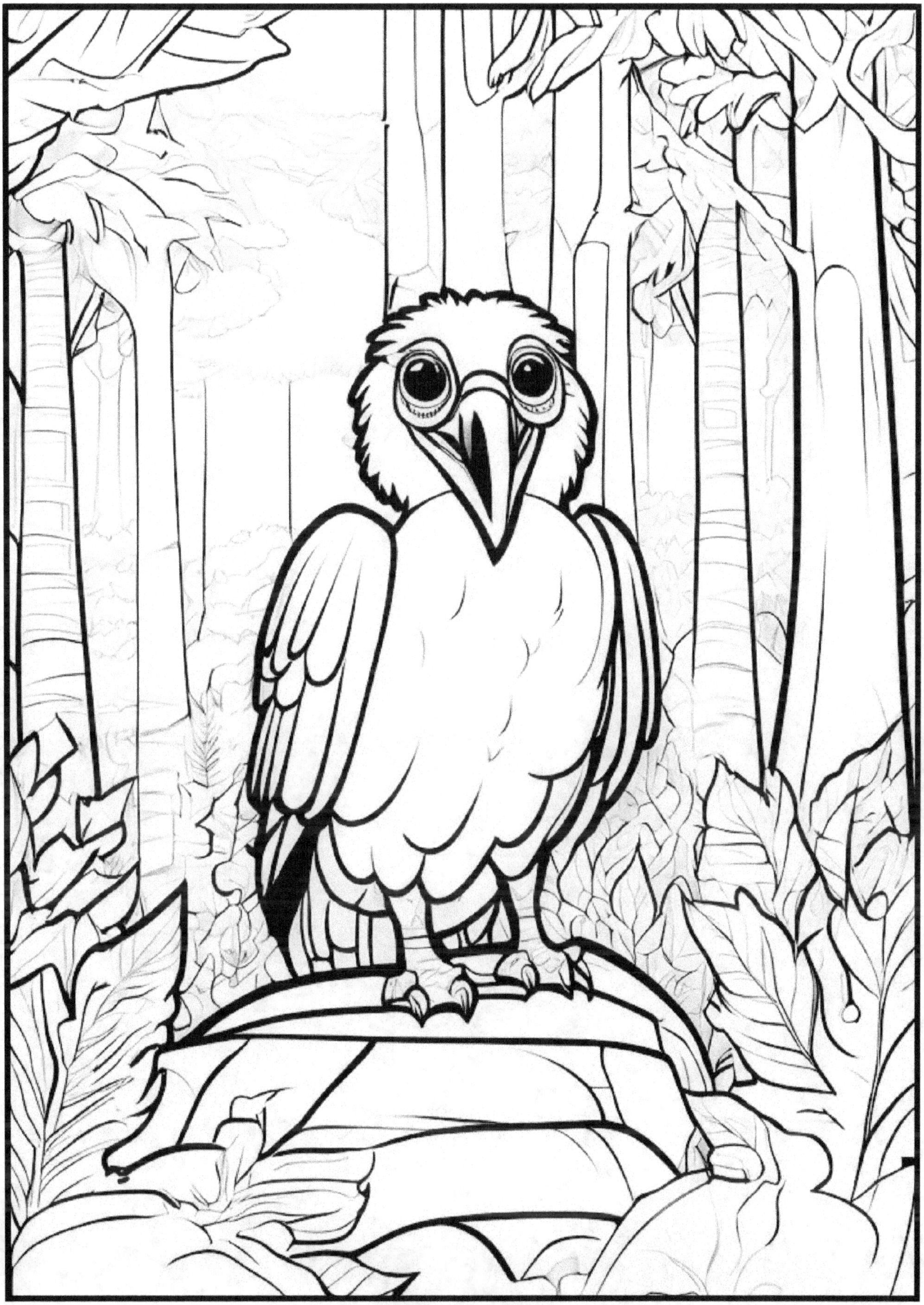

caterpillar

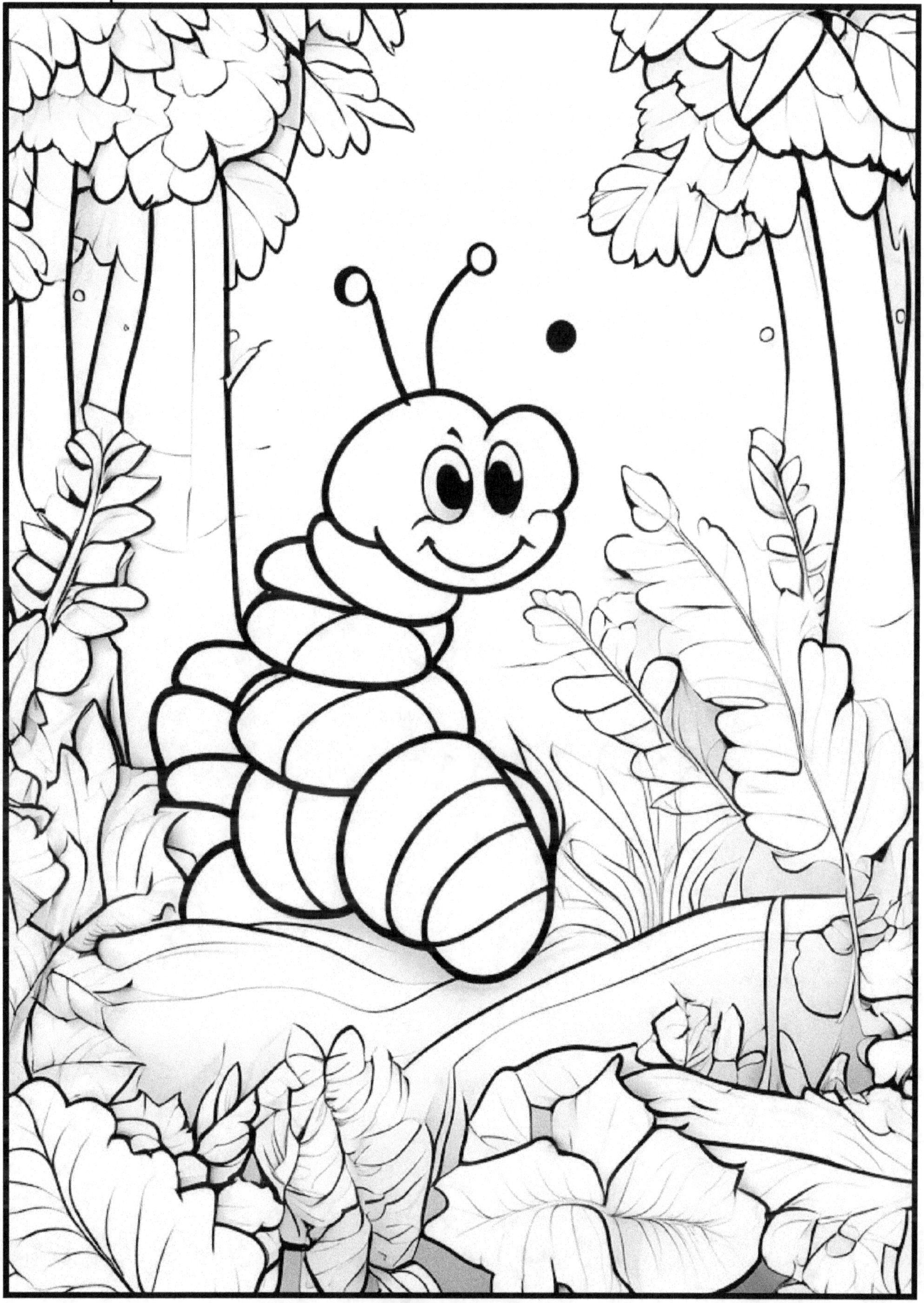

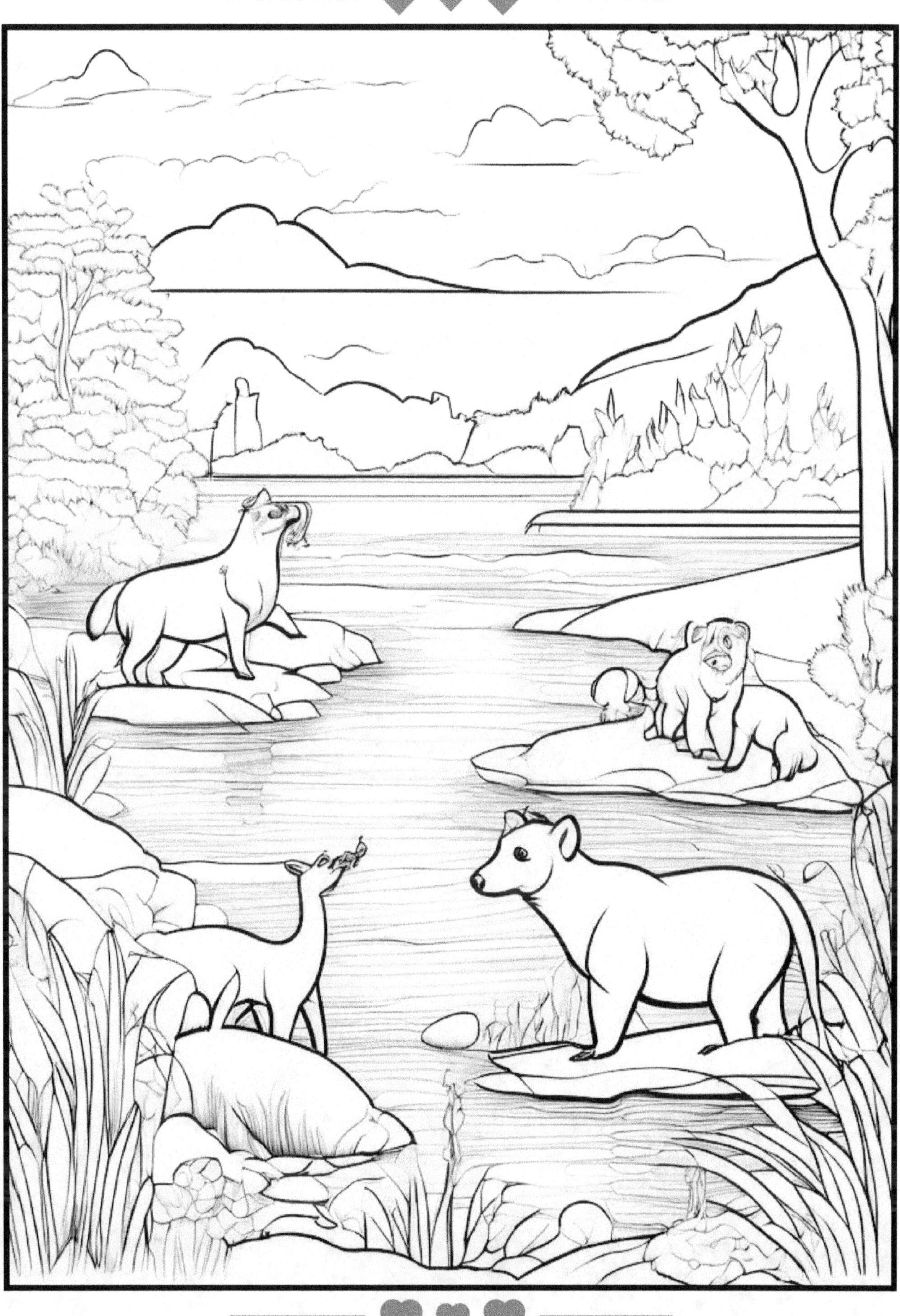

butterfly

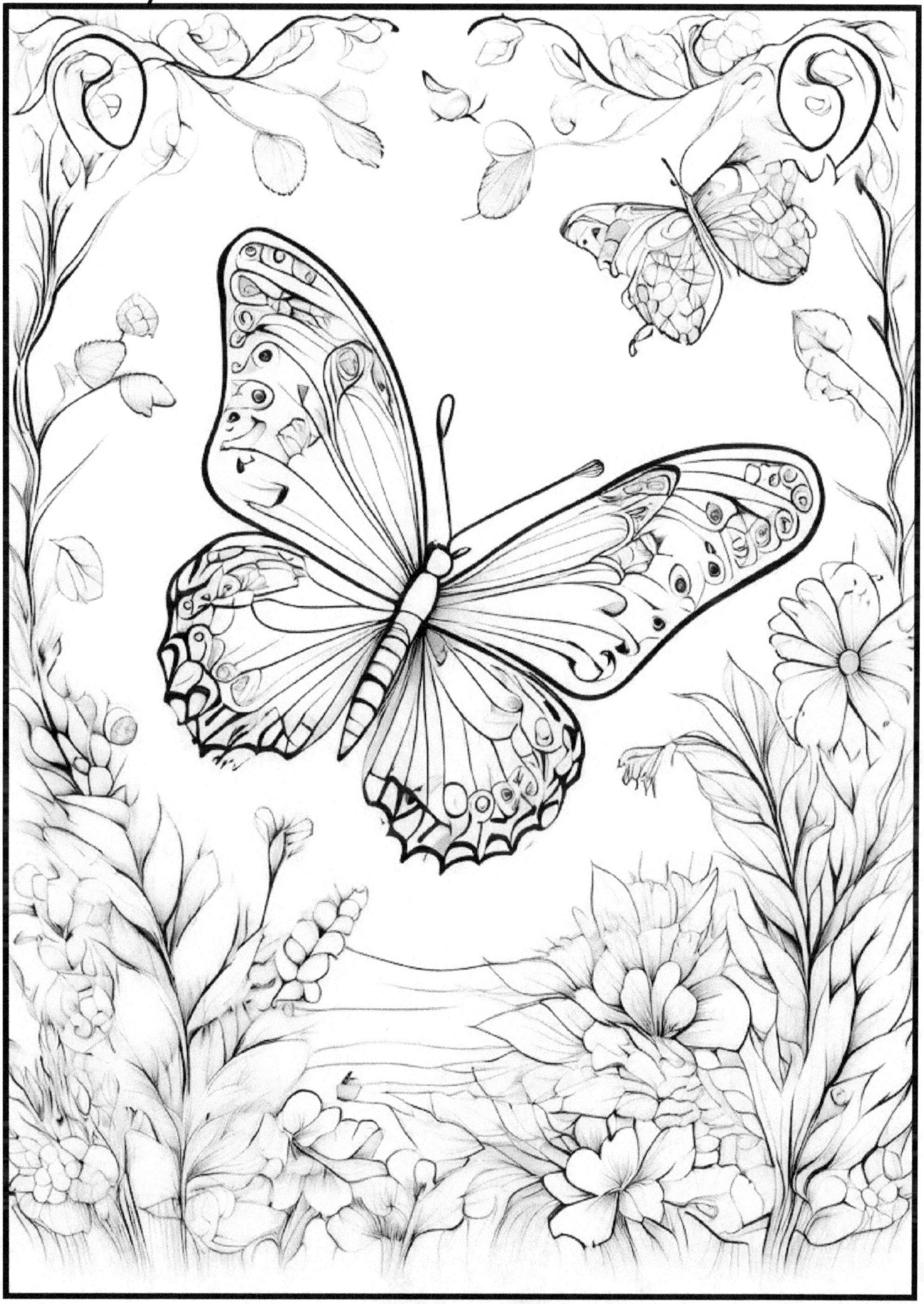

owl

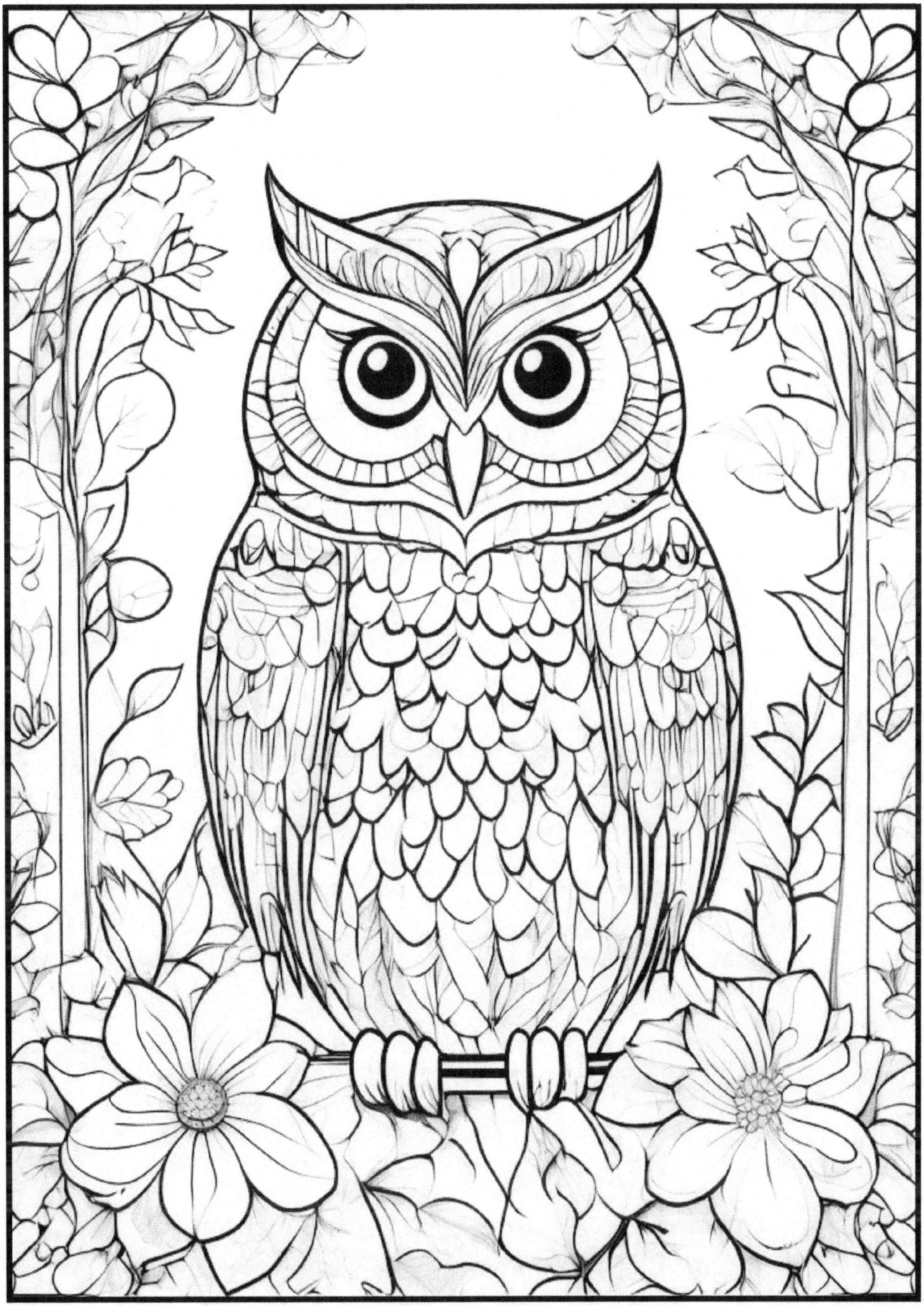

lizard

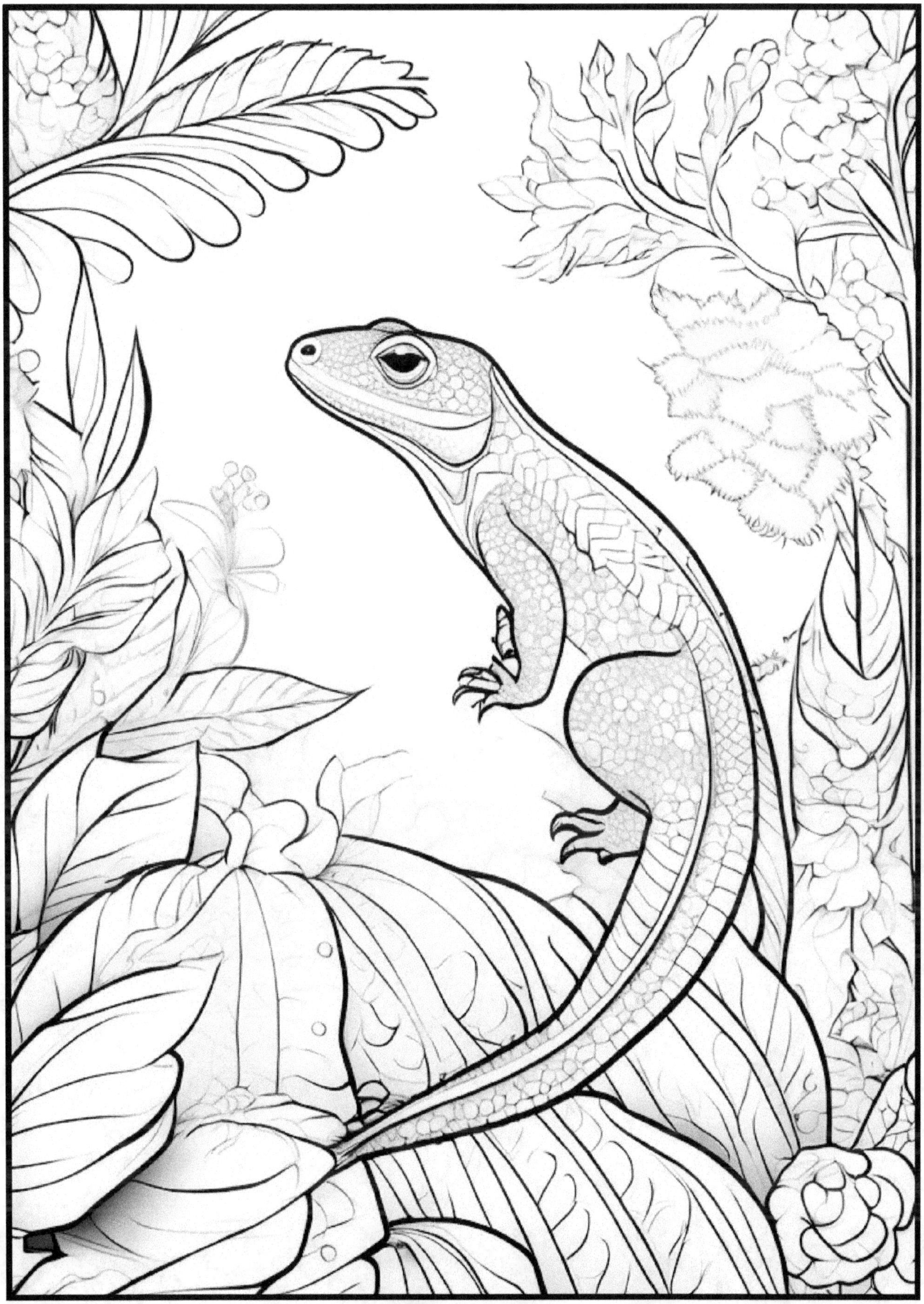

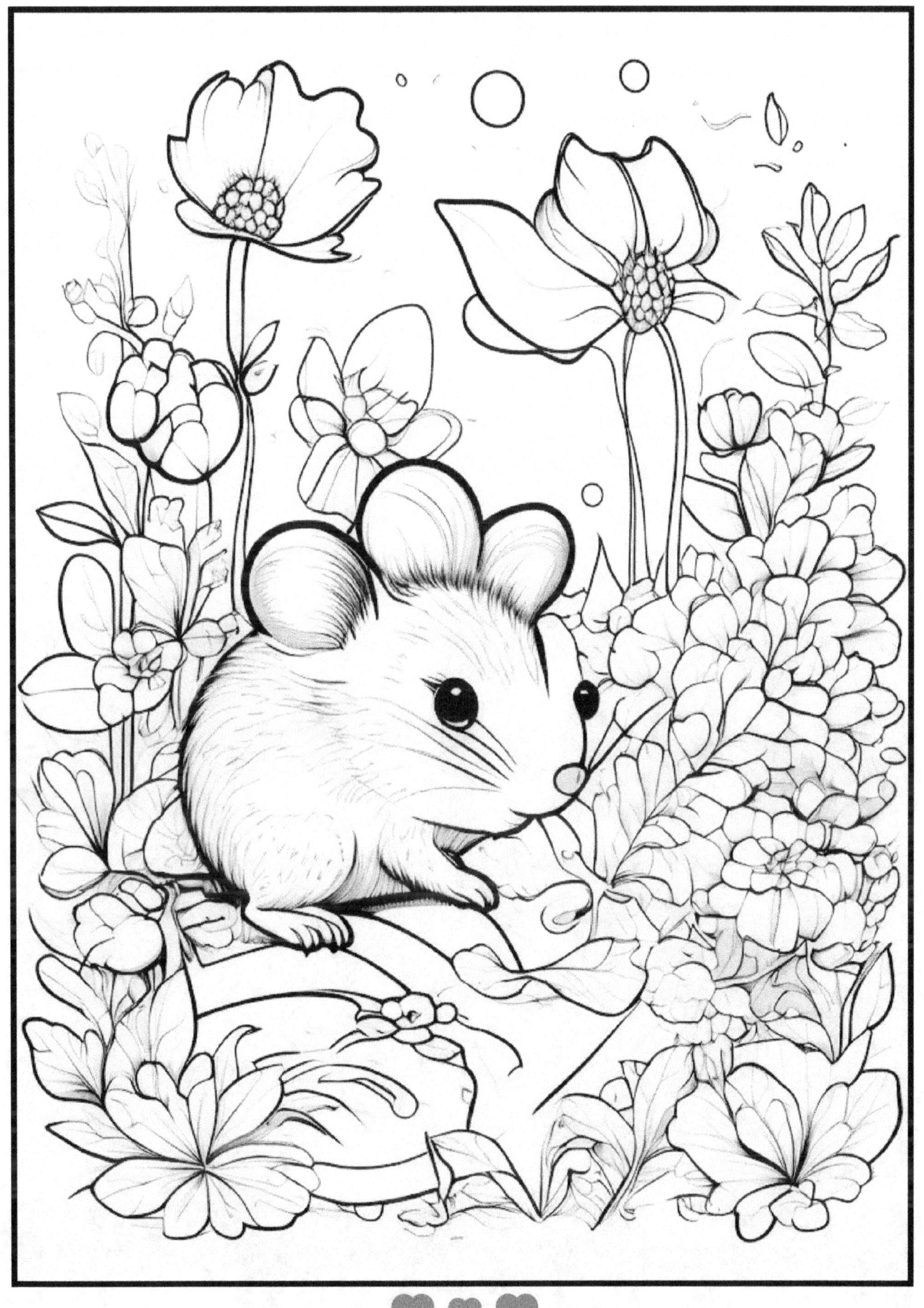

three-toed sloth

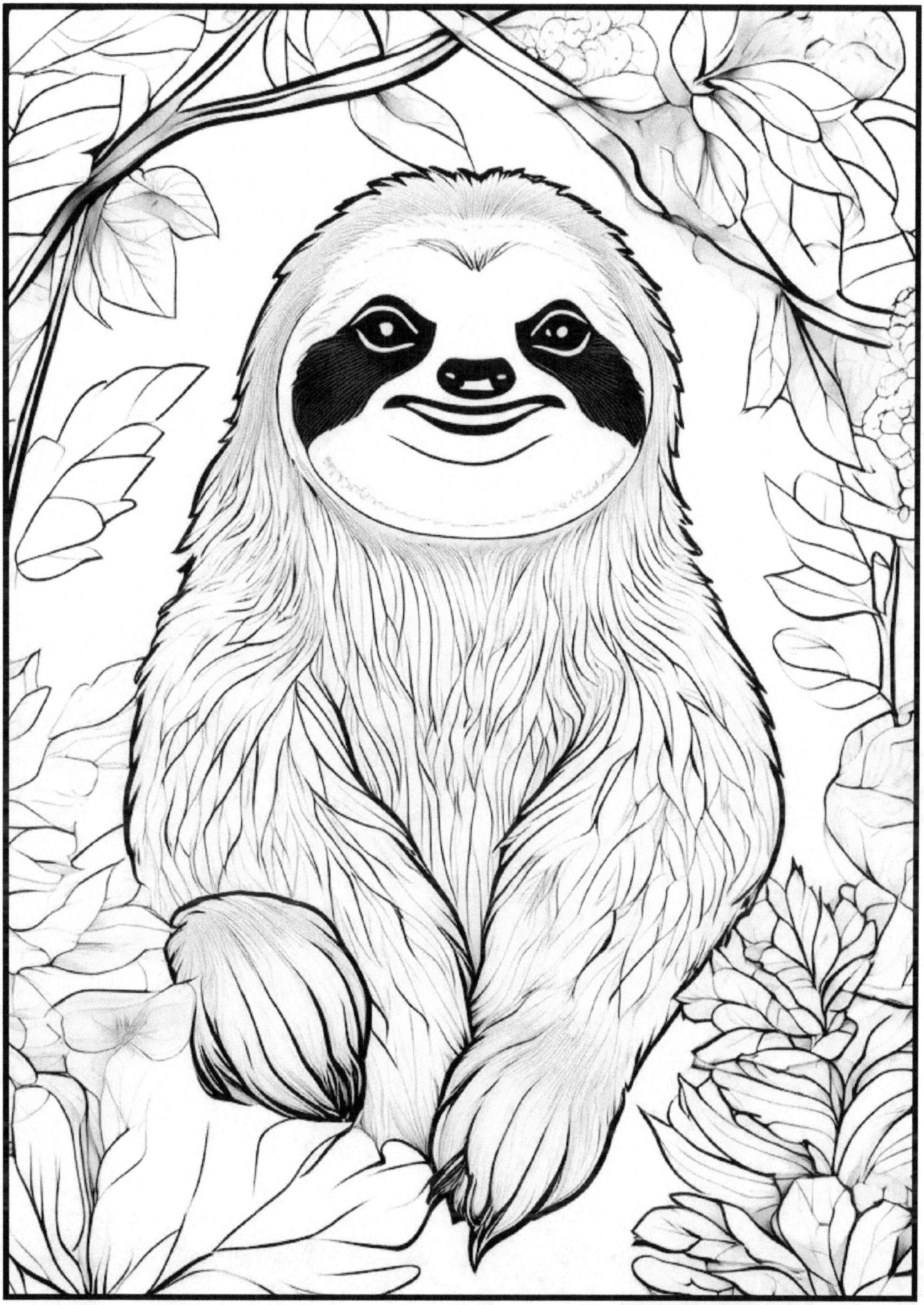

bat

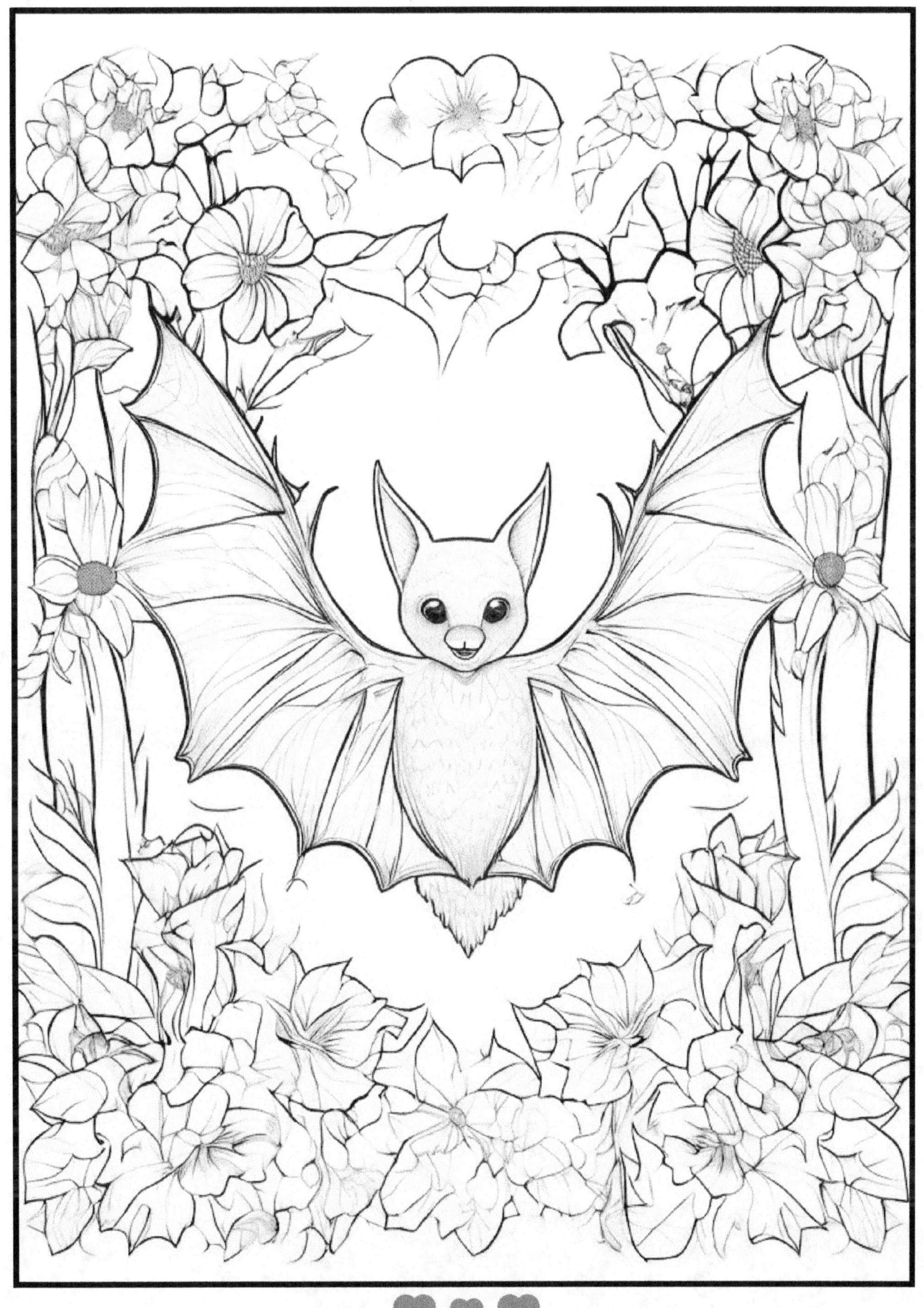

bat

South American tapir

Margay

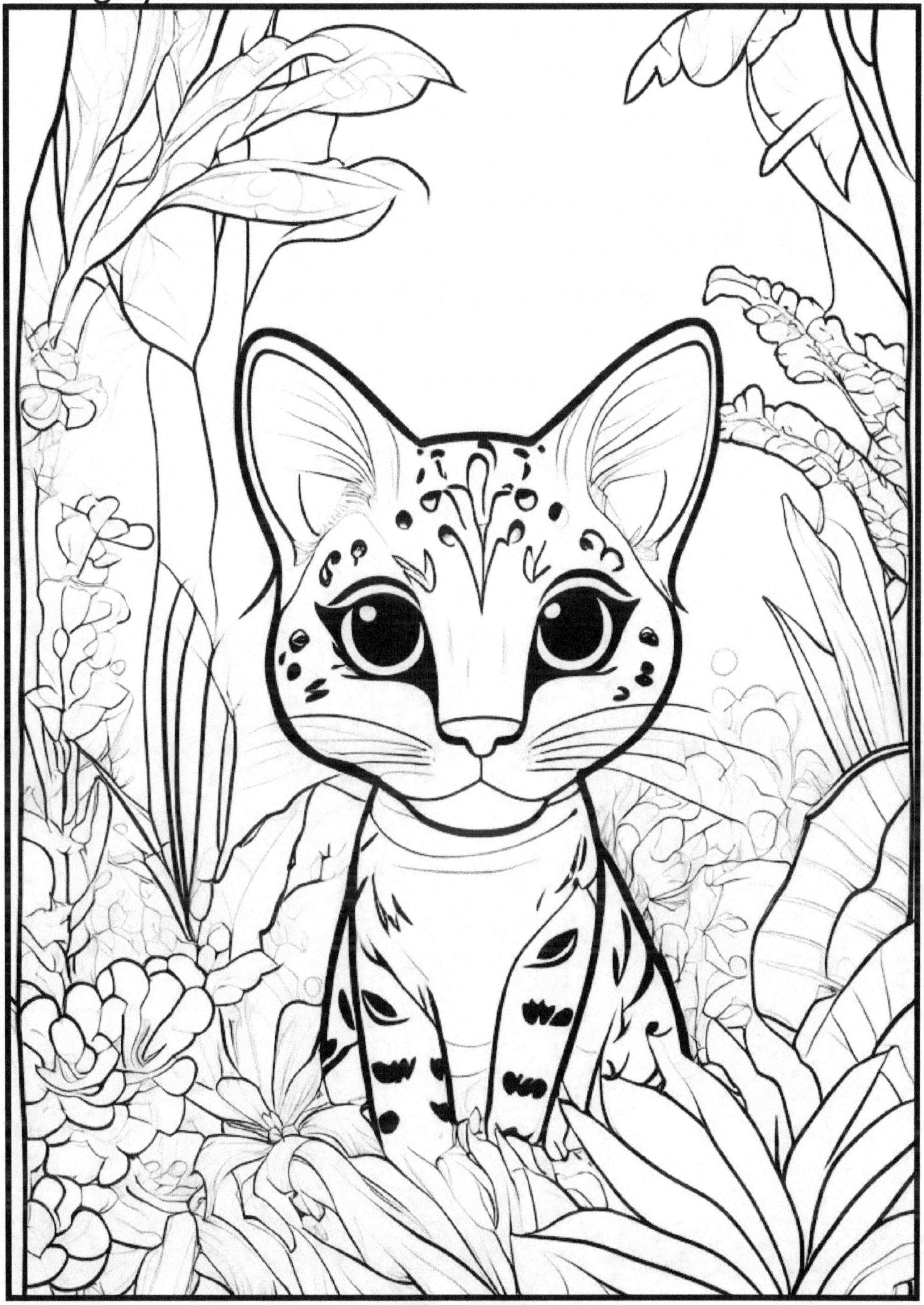

Capybara

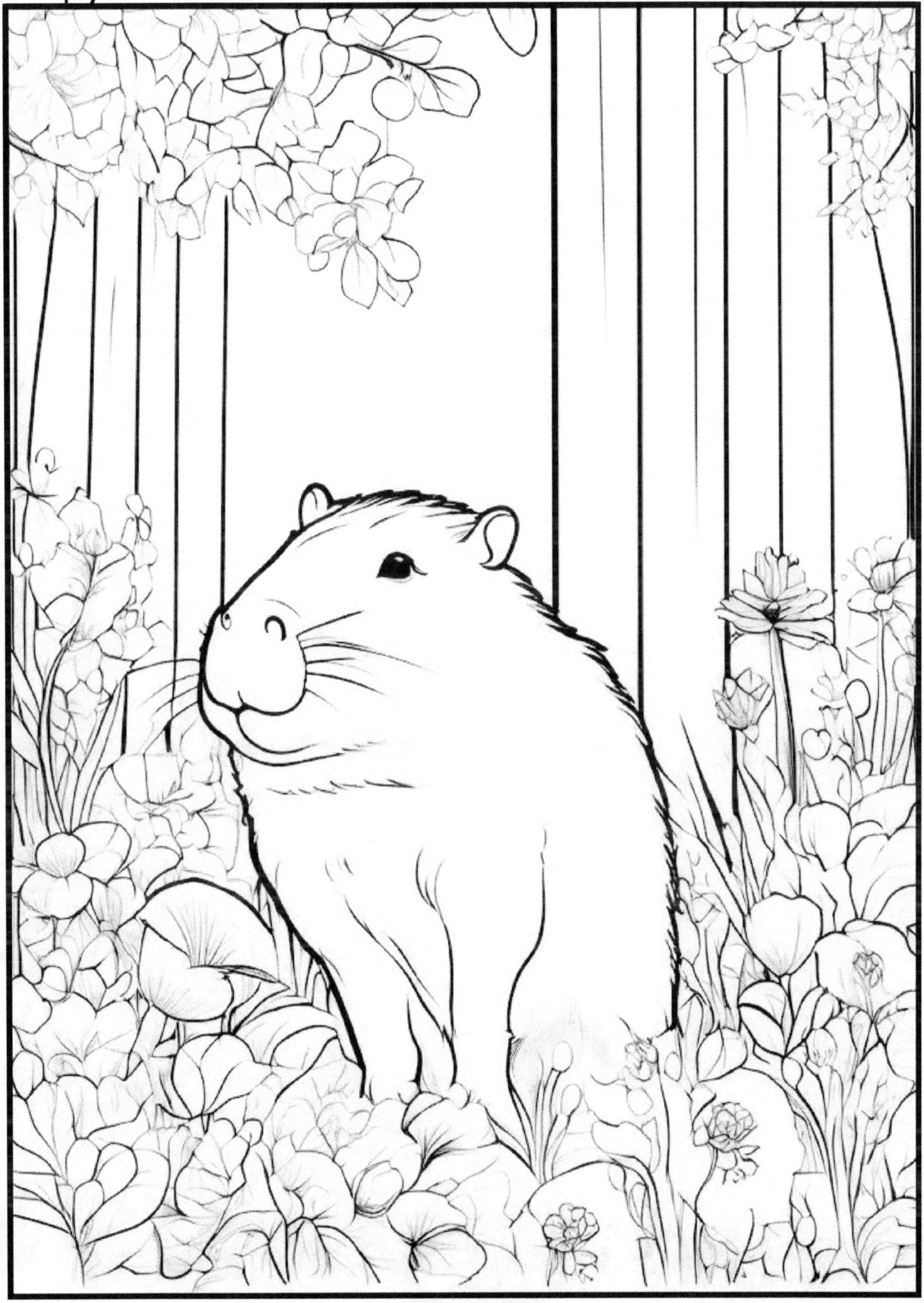

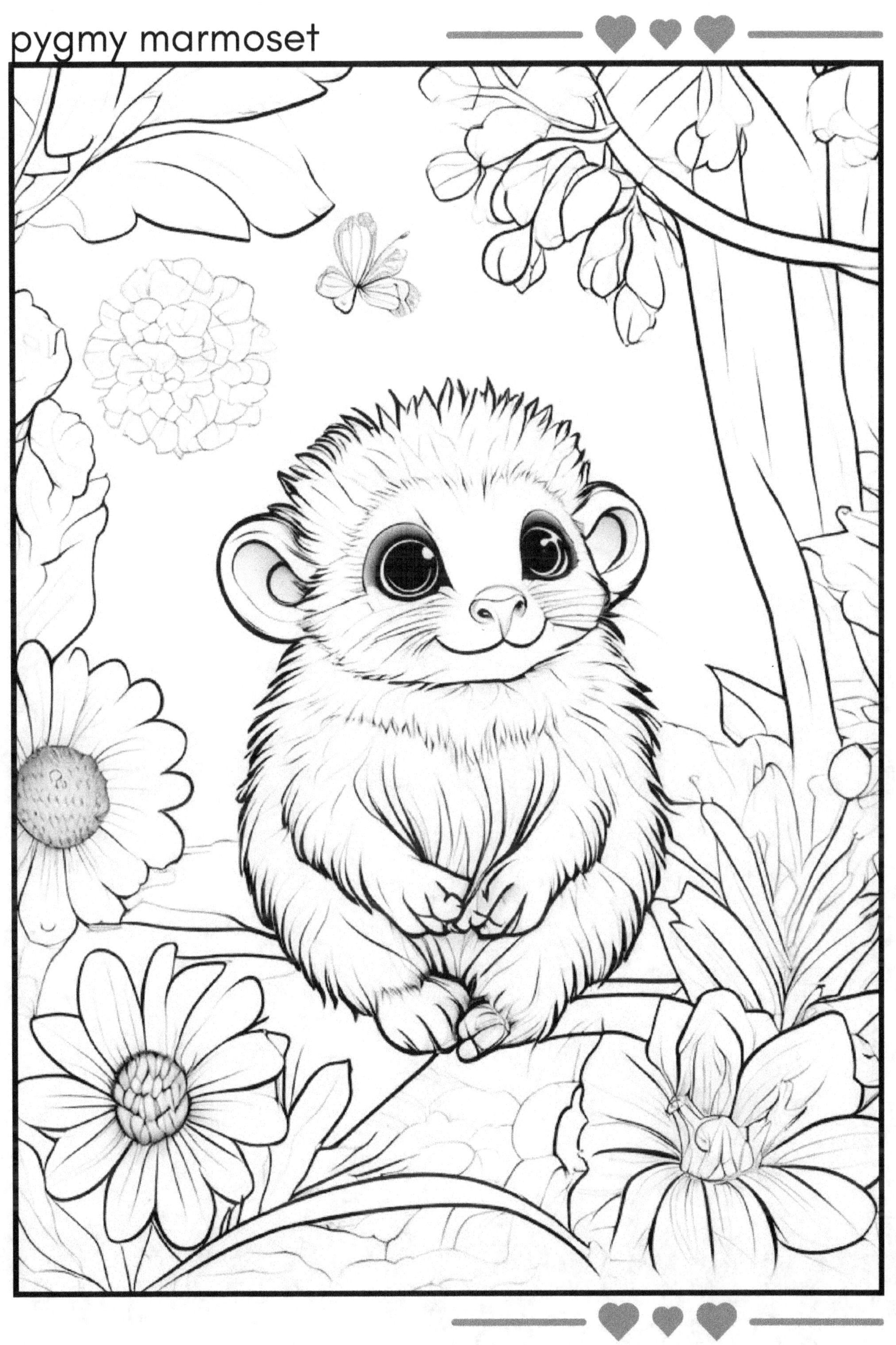

Guanaco

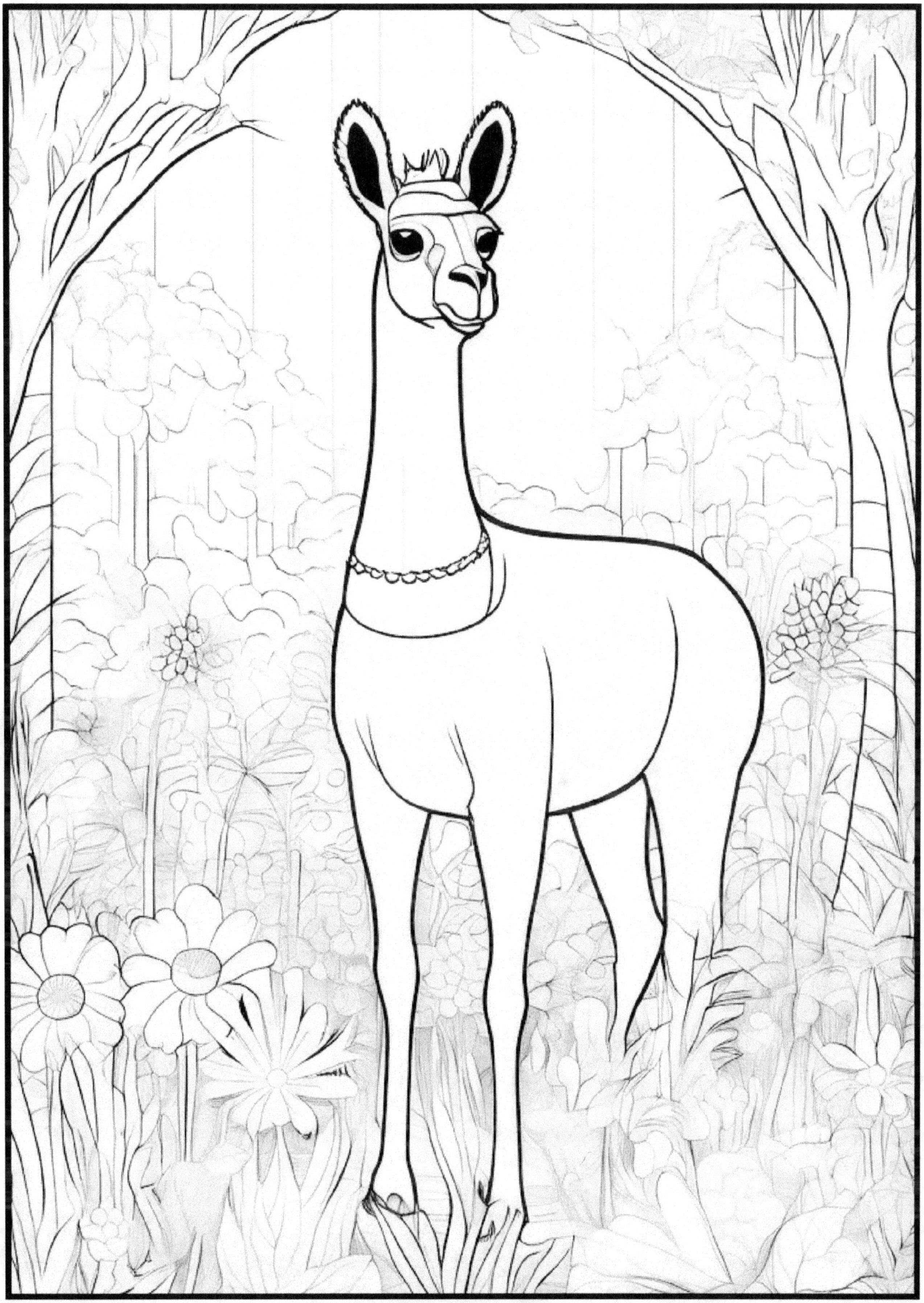

Flamingo

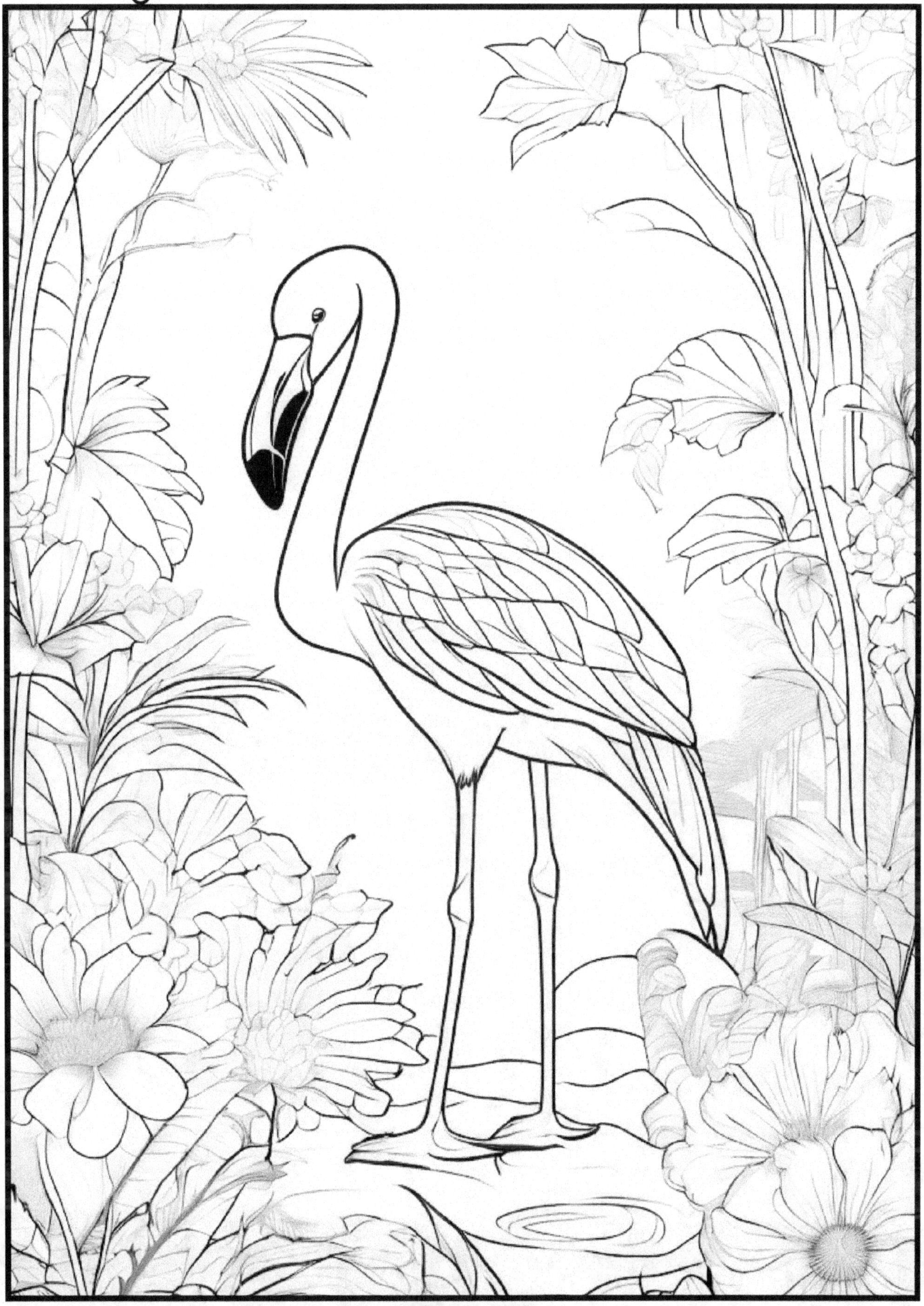

Anteater

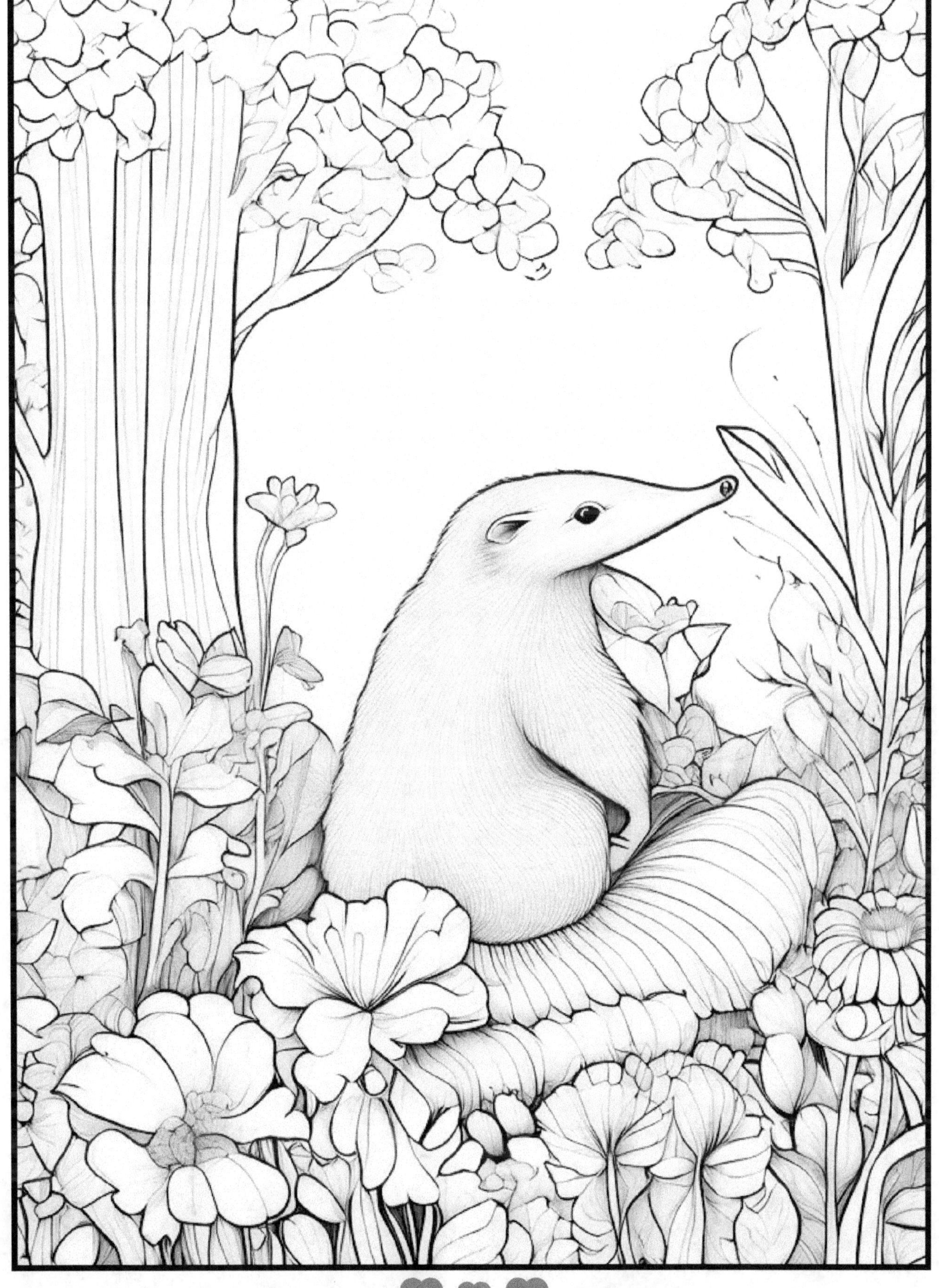

Llama

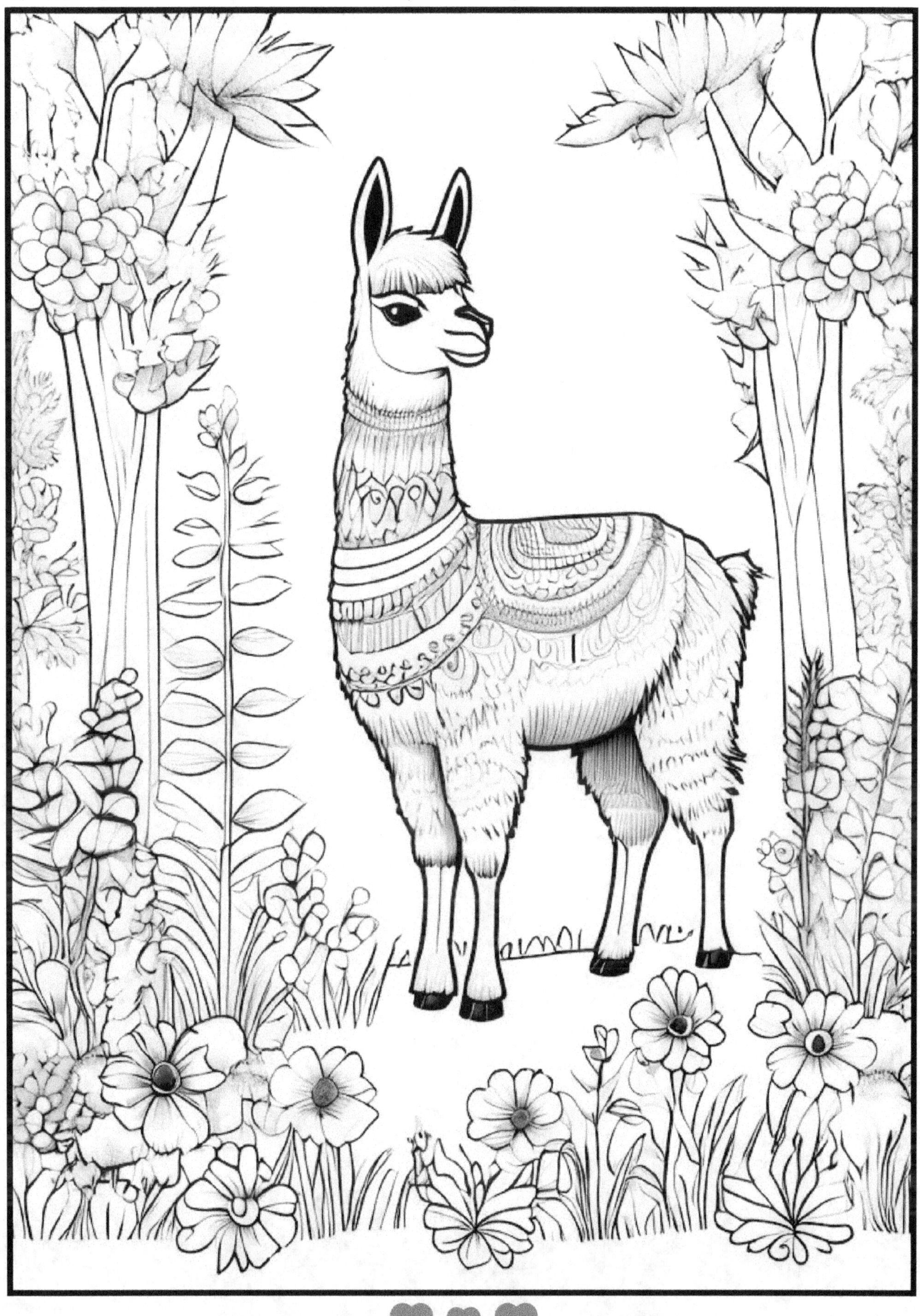

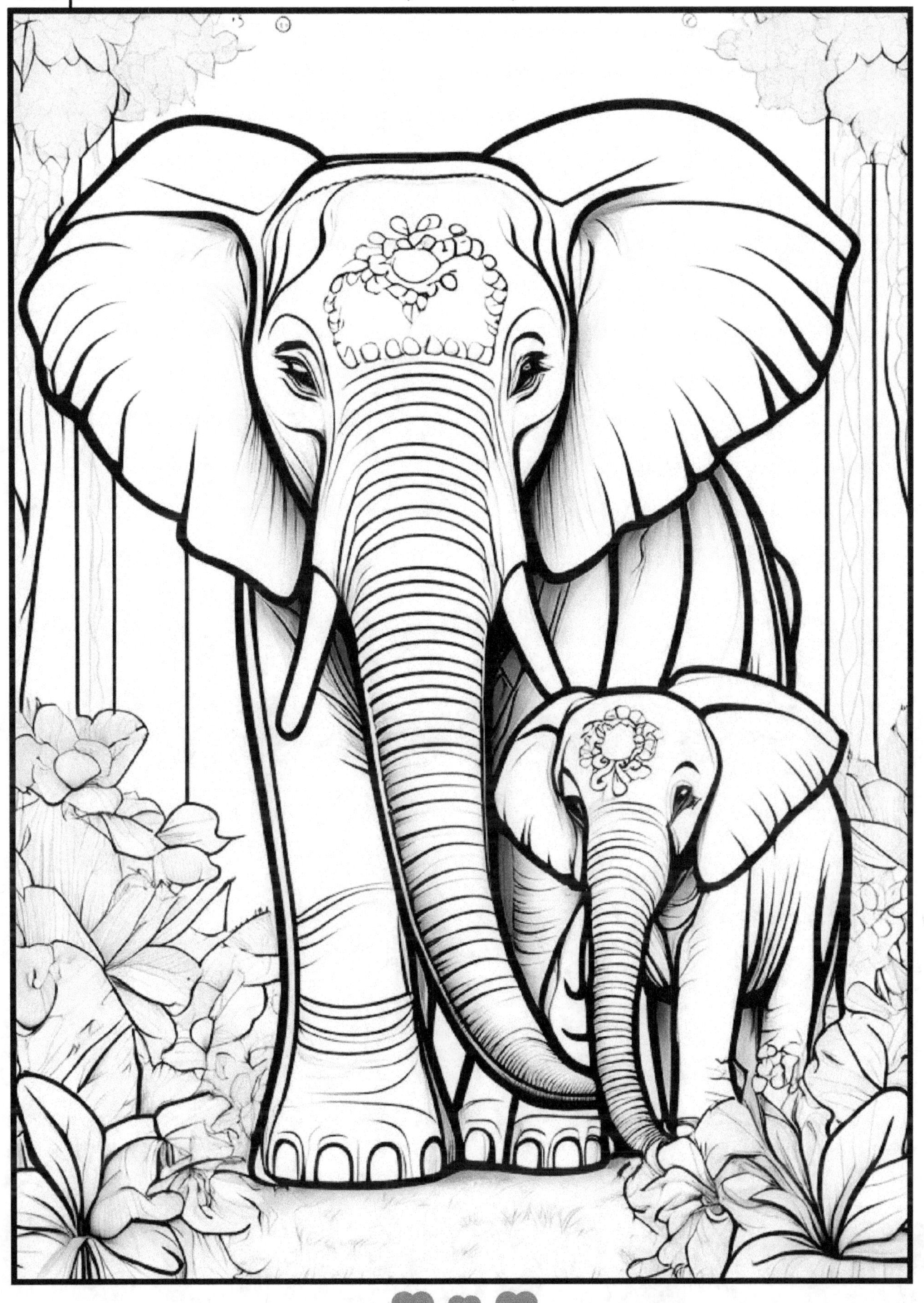

black panther

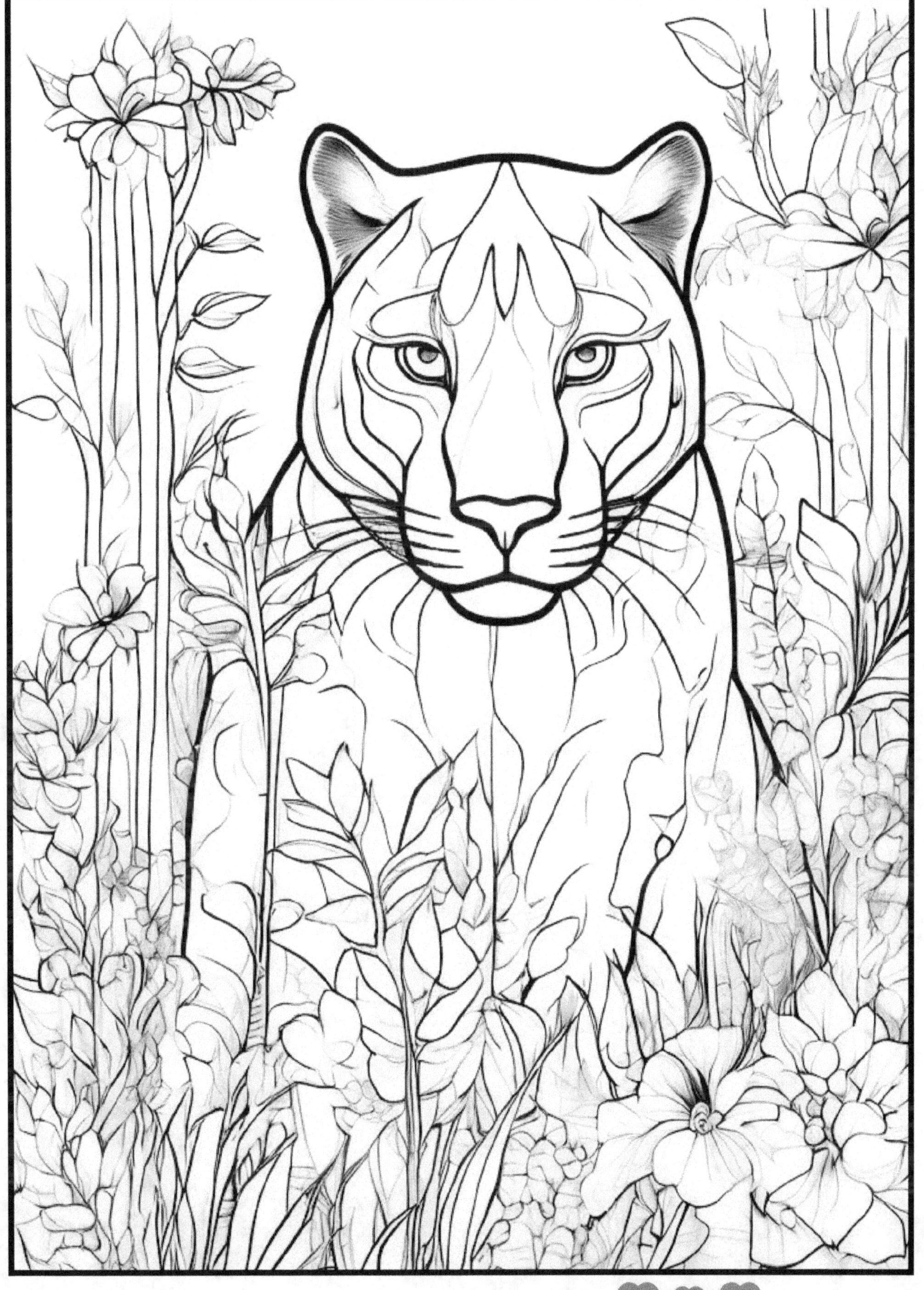

lion

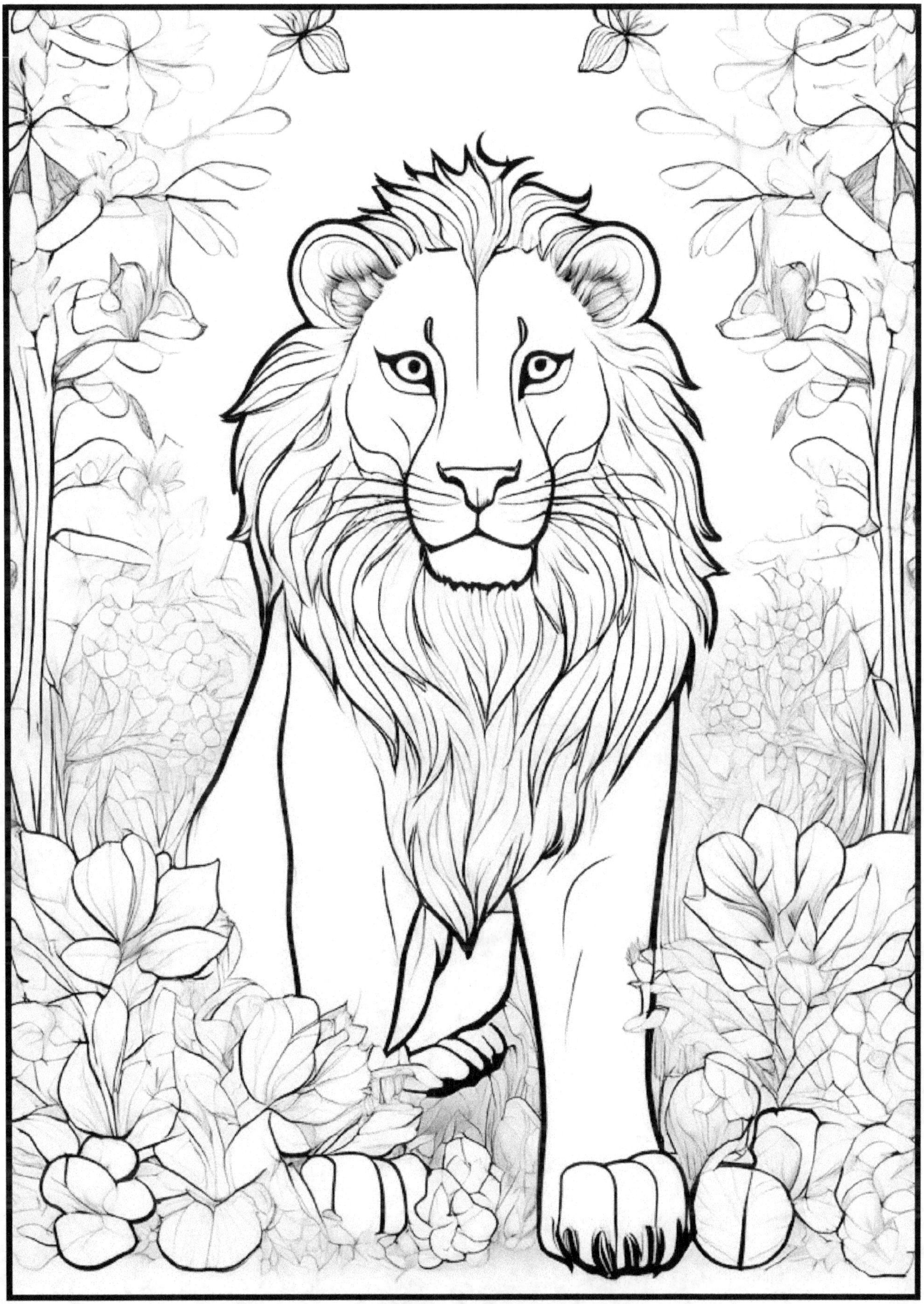

baboon

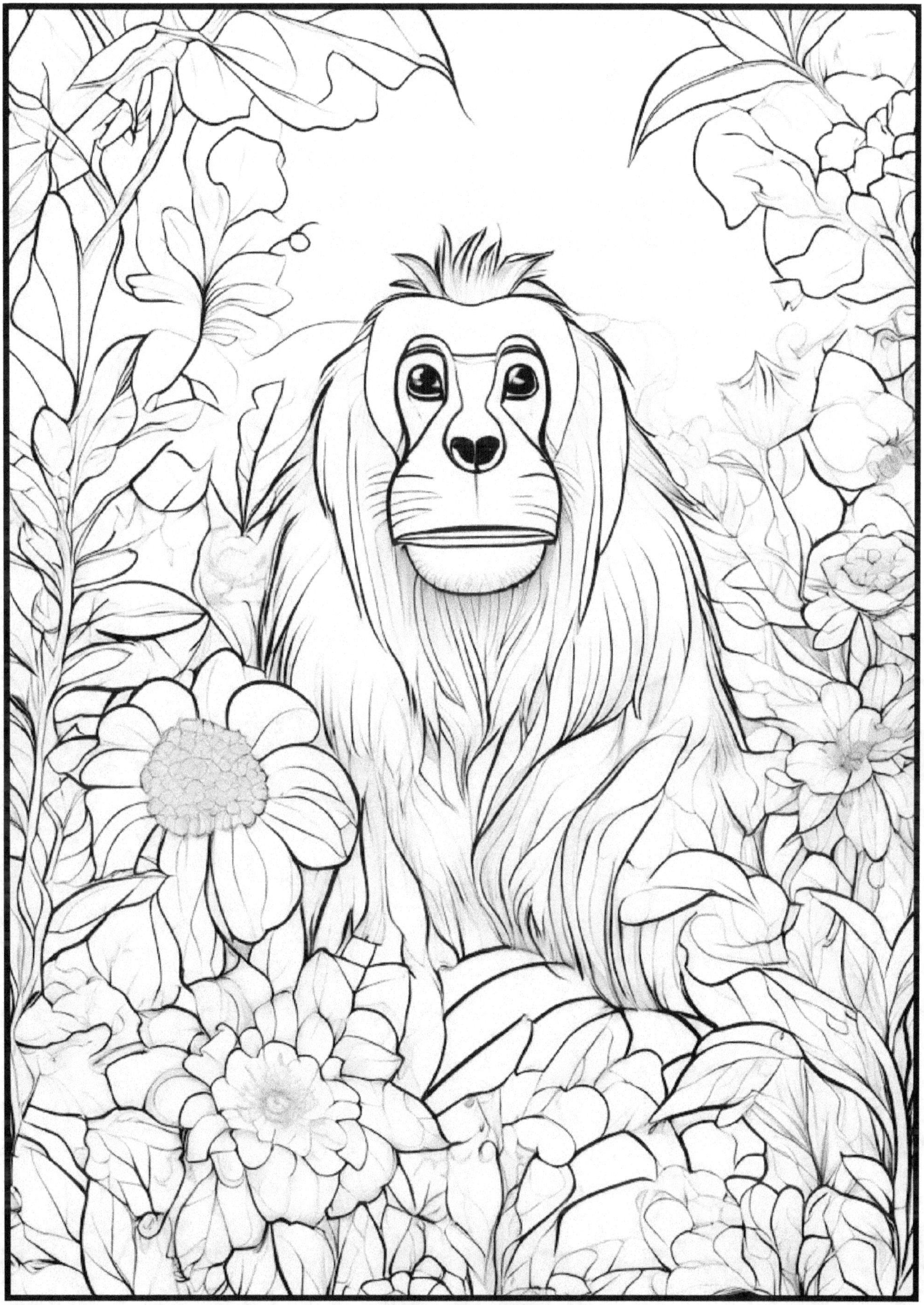

numbat

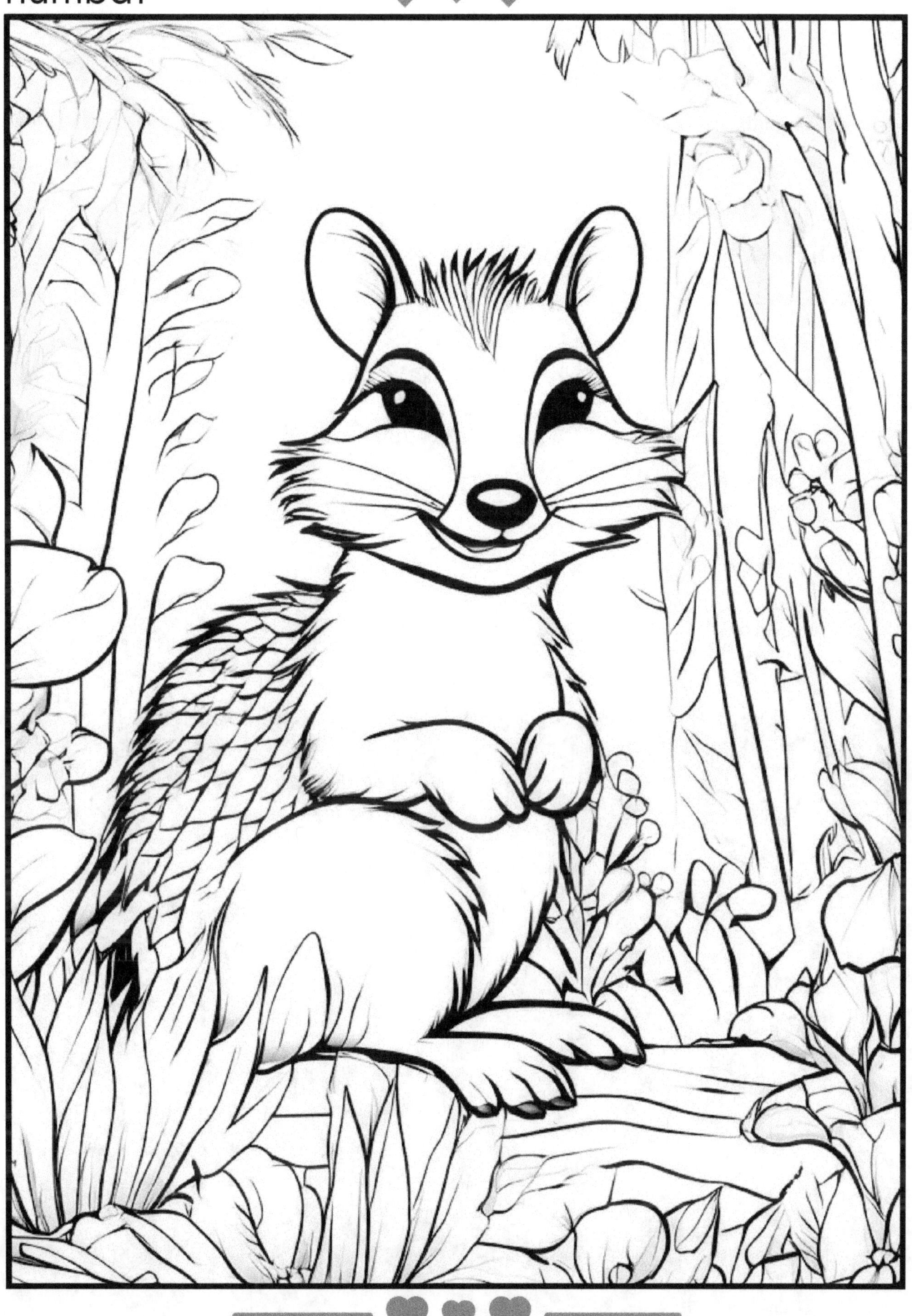

sloth

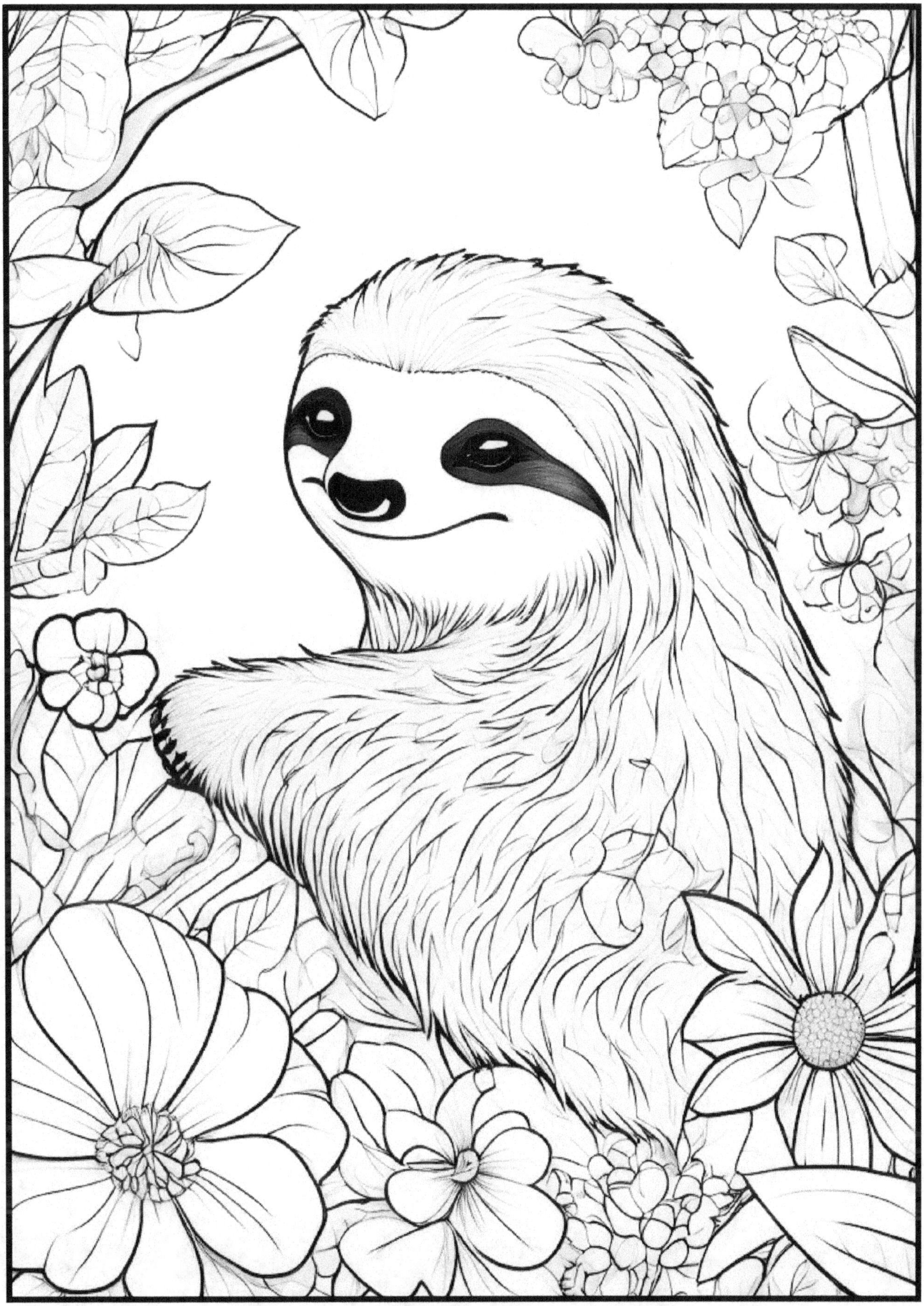

tarsier

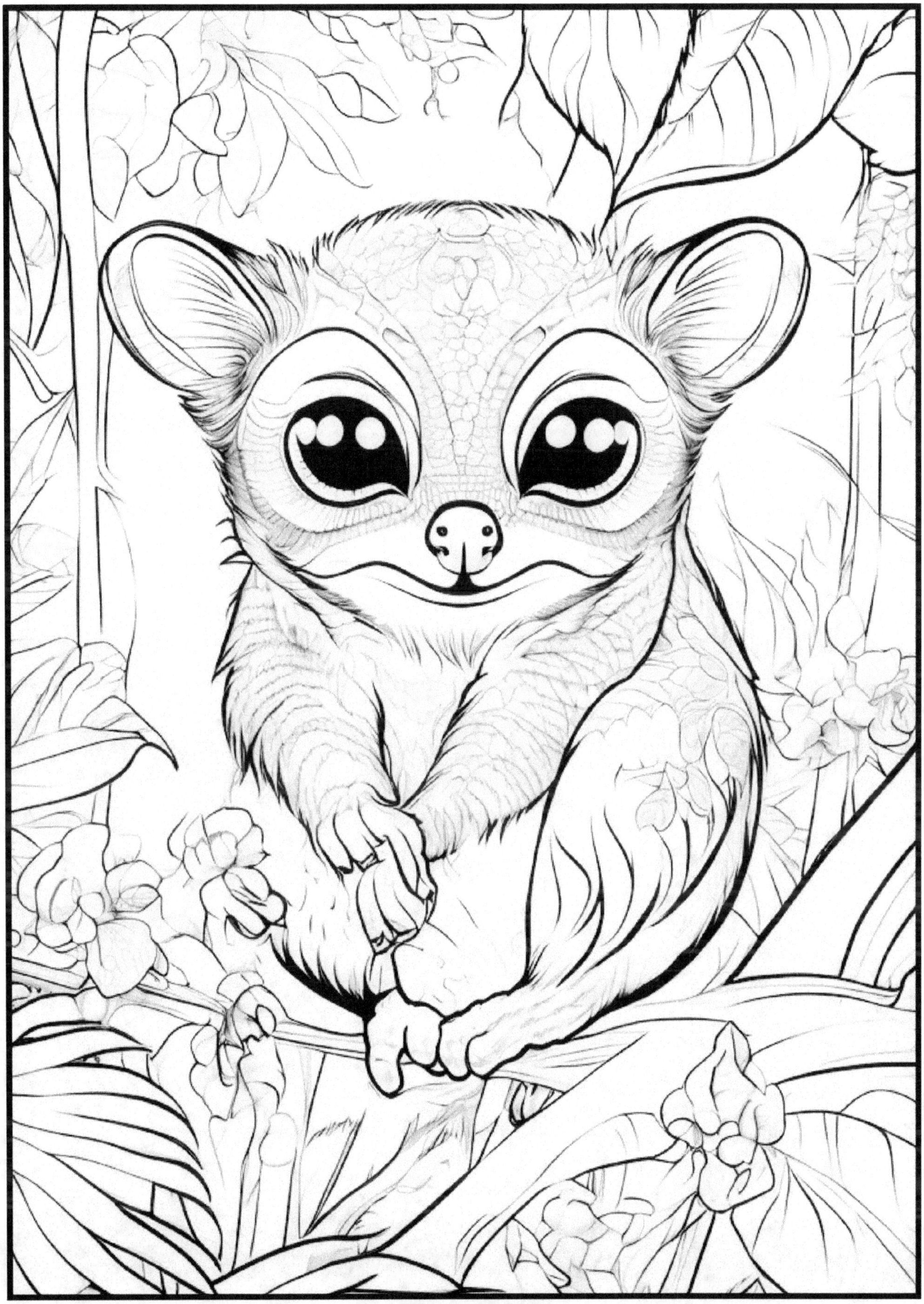

baby owl

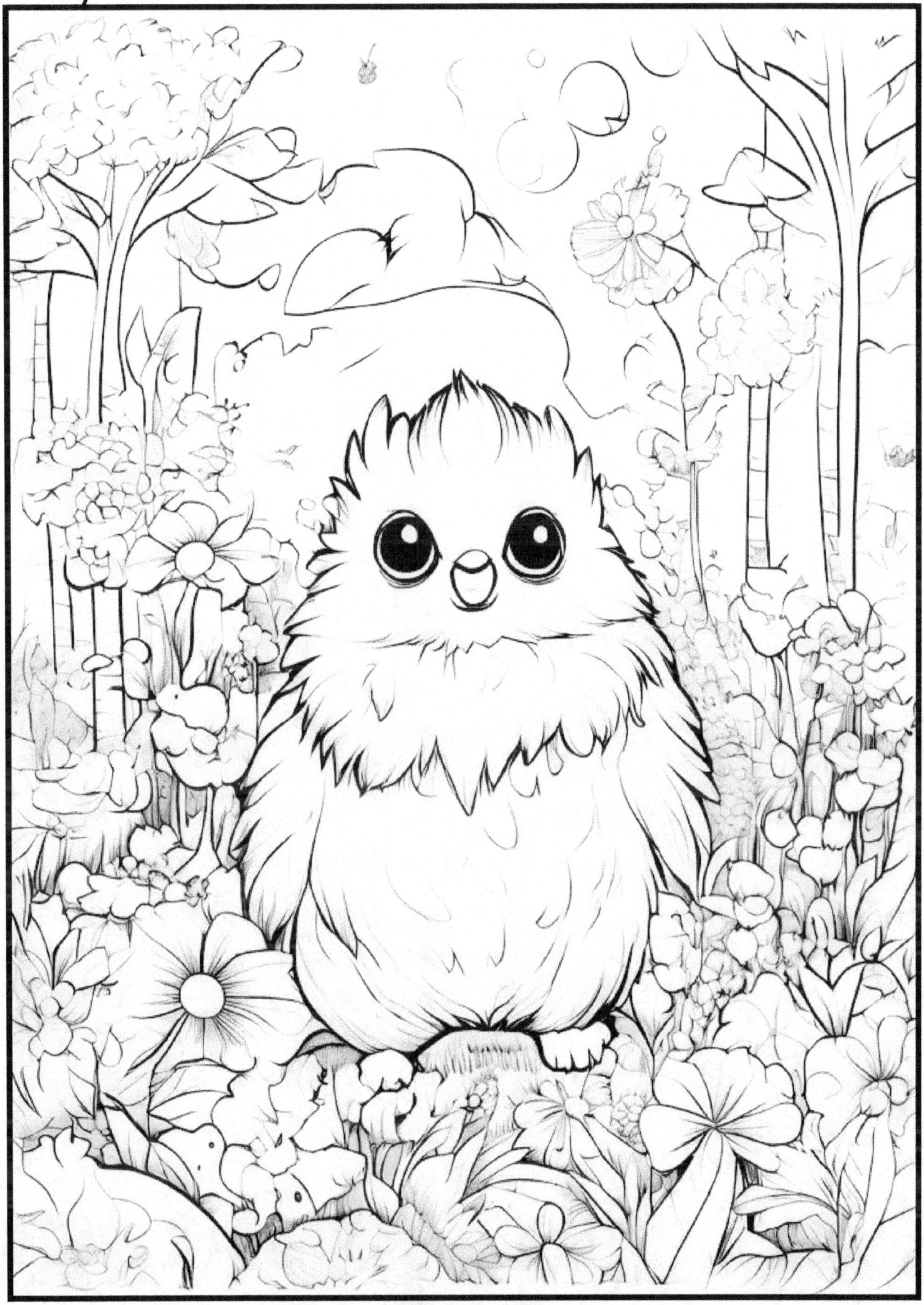

Woodchuck

Woodchuck

mole

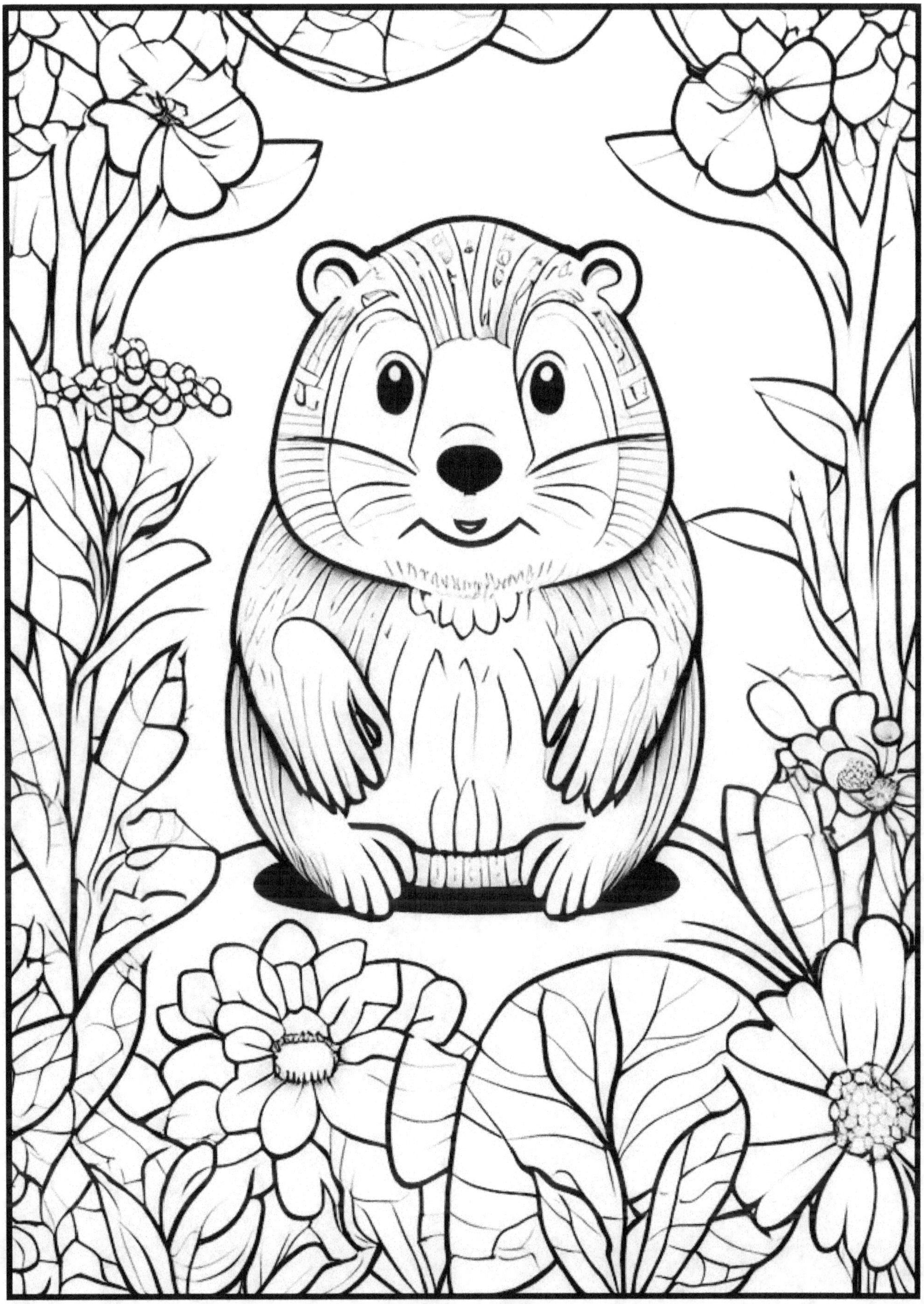

Hummingbird

Tasmania Devil

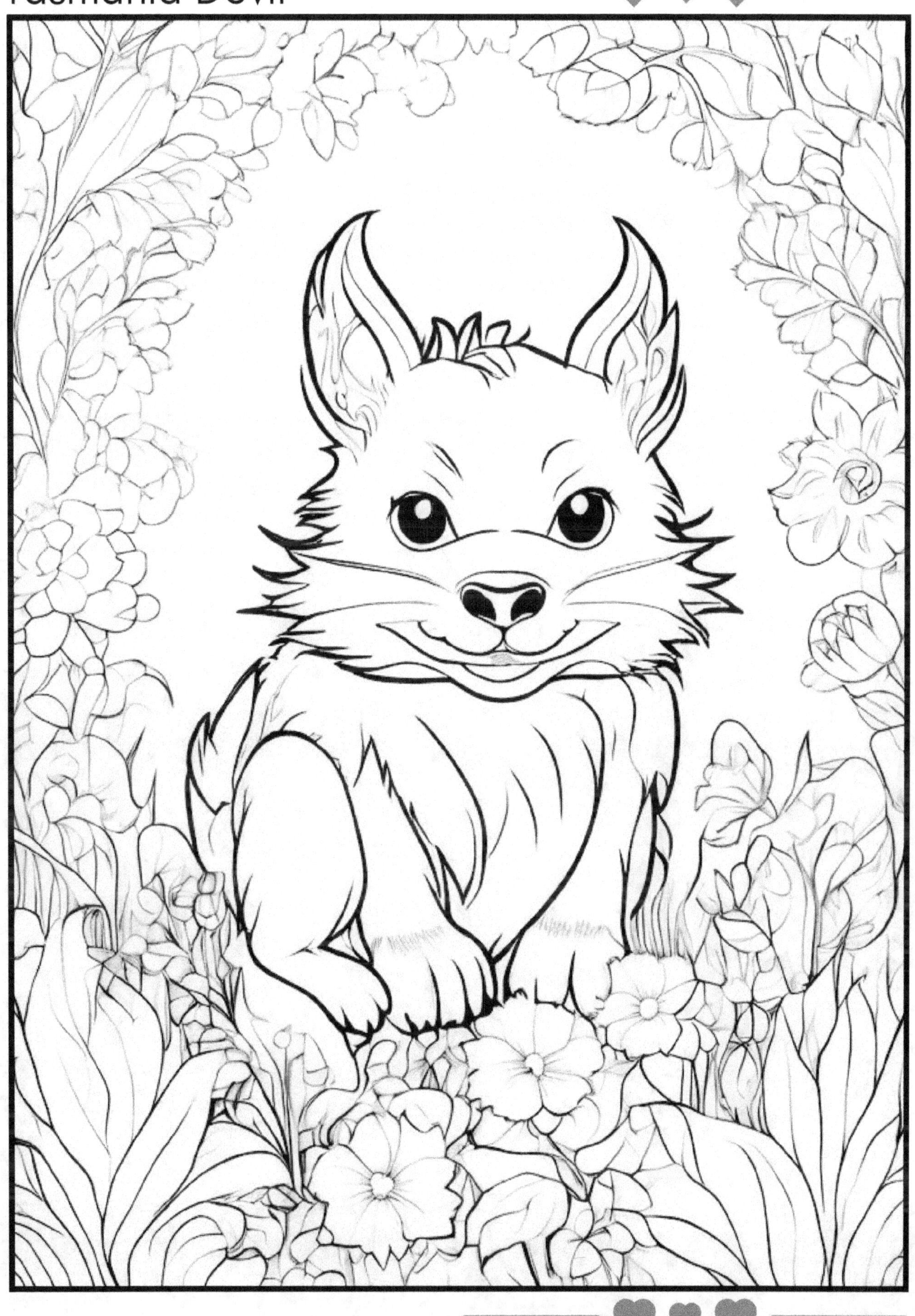